On Your Bike Hertfordshire & Bedfordshire

Audrey Hughes

COUNTRYSIDE BOOKS
NEWBURY, BERKSHIRE

First published 2003

COUNTRYSIDE BOOKS
3 Catherine Road
Newbury, Berkshire

To view our complete range of books,
please visit us at
www.countrysidebooks.co.uk

ISBN 1 85306 795 4

Designed by Graham Whiteman
Maps and photographs by the author
Cover photo supplied by Cyclographic Publications

Typeset by Textype, Cambridge
Produced through MRM Associates Ltd., Reading
Printed in Italy

CONTENTS

AREA MAP SHOWING THE LOCATIONS OF THE RIDES

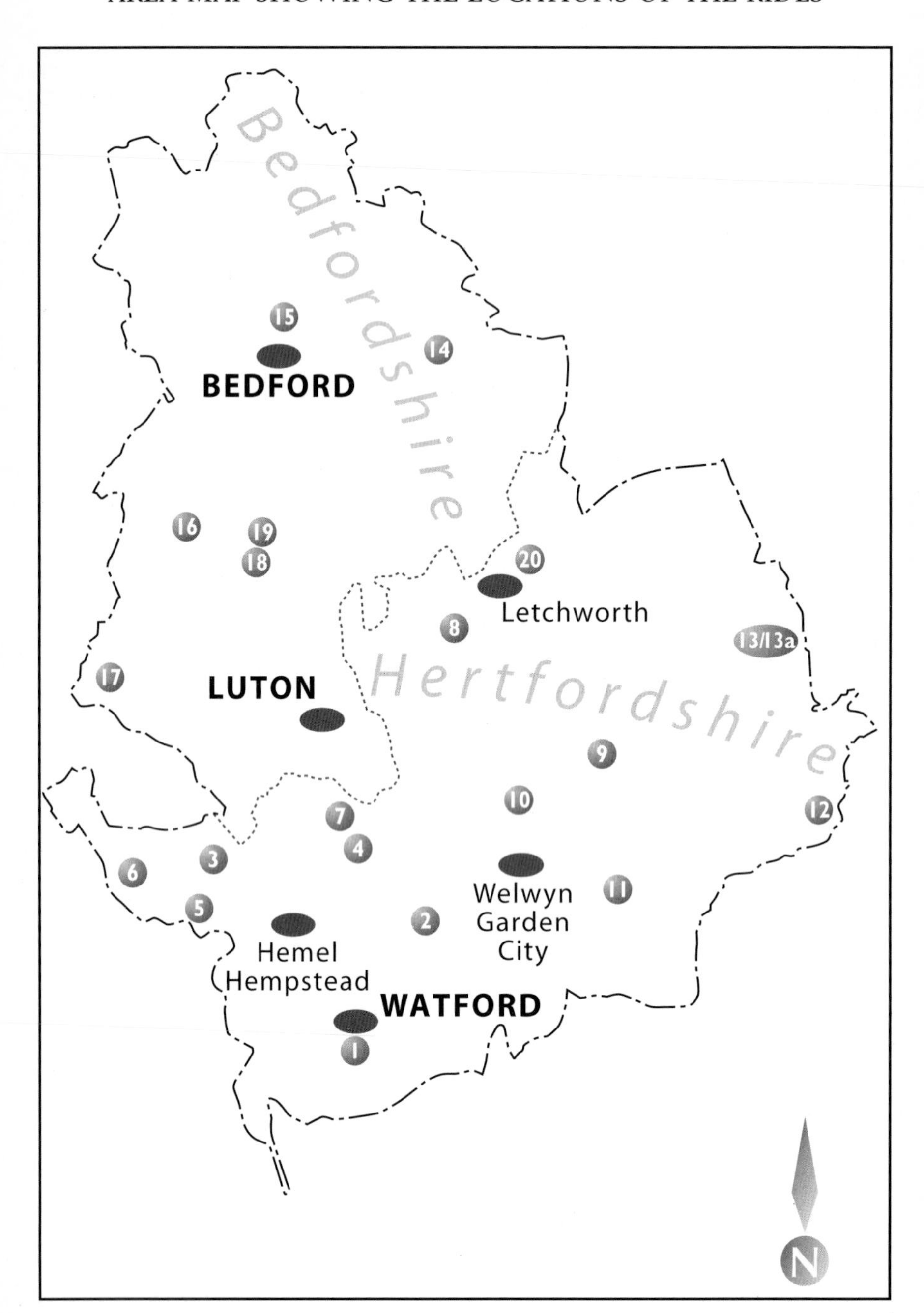

INTRODUCTION

Perhaps Hertfordshire and Bedfordshire are not the counties that first come to mind when planning a cycling trip – too close to London, too built up, too many main roads, too hilly, too flat. But that is all the down side. Hertfordshire is the escape to the country from North London. Bedfordshire is tiny, but full of character. Let the train take the strain and carry you and your bike to country stations. Use those main roads to carry you and your bike quickly to your touring area. Use this book and an Ordnance Survey map to avoid the built up areas, then the hills and valleys fall into place, with many gentle climbs to reach viewpoints, easy rolling countryside that makes you want to go on and on to the next pretty village or welcoming pub, flat lands for huge skies and fresh air. All these are found in Hertfordshire and Bedfordshire.

As for places of interest, we can visit Woburn, one of the major great houses of the country, Old Warden, a great collection of vintage aircraft still able to fly, a wildlife park, wind and water mills, a natural history museum, historic airfields, a narrow gauge railway and innumerable villages with their own styles of architecture and local histories.

In the past there have been many famous people living in the area, changing the lives of those around them. St Alban upheld Christianity and was martyred here. John Bunyan preached and wrote his books and was imprisoned here. Bridgwater built his canals here. George Bernard Shaw wrote and cycled here and Lord Rothschild harnessed zebras and drove them round his park here. And the ordinary people who lived in these counties have all left something in the way they kept their homes, attended their churches and carried out their work.

You may not find the solitude of faraway places, but once you leave those main roads behind there are delightful lanes meandering through pasture, woodland, parkland and farm fields. There are off-road trails and railway paths, country parks and canalsides to help you get away from traffic fumes and road rage, and just enjoy cycling.

Audrey Hughes

GUIDE TO USING THIS BOOK

Each route is preceded by information to help you:

The **number of miles** is indicated for the main route. Detour or short-cut mileage is given in the text. Distances are measured on the map.

The brief **introduction** gives a broad picture of the area to be covered and mentions particular features.

The **maps** listed are all Ordnance Survey Landranger series (1¼ inches to the mile/2 cm to the kilometre) and it is recommended that you carry them with you to augment the information on the sketch maps. The Explorer series maps (2½ inches to the mile) give much more detail, but are relatively bulky to carry on a longer ride.

The grid reference for the suggested **starting point** is given, as well as car parking details. It is often possible to park at a public house you may be returning to for a drink or a meal, but only if you ask first. The leaflet *Cycling by Train,* available to members of the Cycle Touring Club (CTC) (telephone: 0870 873 0060), gives extremely helpful guidance to the various rail companies' rules on the acceptance of bicycles. It is always possible to join the routes at any convenient point.

The names of public houses, restaurants and cafés are given as guidance to places of **refreshment**. Many of these have been visited, but it is not possible to try them all, and landlords, opening hours and menus may change. On a sunny summer day a picnic may be the best lunch. REMEMBER – you must not ride under the influence of drink or drugs.

THE ROUTES

It is a good idea to read right through the route before you set out so as to note places where you may wish to stop and explore. Remember that things can change – pubs close, tracks deteriorate or roads close for repair. Whilst every care has been taken to be accurate, things may not be quite as written.

The route directions have been written as concisely as possible so as to be memorable over short stretches. The off-road sections have been ridden in variable weather conditions and are reasonably easy. The turns and safety warnings are given in **bold type**. Remember if you explore off the road that surfaces may be very poor in the winter and that you should not cycle on footpaths. Cyclists are allowed on bridleways, byways, roads used as public paths (RUPPS) and special cycle routes. Local Tourist Information offices can often offer cycling routes and maps of cycle paths.

In some routes variations have been given, but it is possible to lengthen or shorten any of your rides by using the map. Be prepared to walk where indicated, as safety is most important and there are one or two bridges and embankments where steps will be found.

Notes on places of interest, architecture, history, etc are given at the end of each route.

SAFETY

Before cycling anywhere make sure your bicycle is in good condition. Again CTC members have access to a comprehensive leaflet, *Get into Cycle Touring,* which covers the subject (see above for phone number). At the least, make sure tyres and brakes are in really good condition, check bars, saddle and wheels for loose nuts and carry your luggage on the bike rather than on your back if possible. Make sure you have a spare inner tube and puncture outfit and that you know how to use it. Thin rubber gloves and a packet of cleansing tissues are a welcome luxury. Remember your padlock in case you leave your bike unattended.

Always be in control of your bike. Remember the lanes you enjoy are also those used by horse riders and often walkers. Talk to the horse if you approach from behind and be prepared to stop if it is frightened. Speak in a friendly manner to walkers and to fishermen on towpaths. Use a bell politely or call out in good time.

Wear comfortable clothing and choose light colours, particularly if you are likely to be out after dark, when you should also be using good quality lights. It is also worth using a rear light in fog. Padded shorts make a lot of difference to comfort and a breathable waterproof is almost essential in this country. Shoes should be strong enough to walk in, where necessary. A stiff sole is preferable on a longer ride. Make sure you have no dangling clothing or straps that could foul the wheels or transmission. Carry a drink, water is fine, all year round. Drink little and often – it can make a great difference to your feeling of well-being. It is also a good idea to carry some food; a snack or fruit will take you several miles if your favoured pub is out of action. You may choose to wear a helmet and it is important for children, but remember that it can protect your head in a tumble but not your body in a more severe accident. Carry a small first aid kit and sun protection. Lip salve is good protection all the year. A cycle computer is useful for checking distances and, in conjunction with the map, can help with the route finding.

The routes in this book have been cycled for pleasure over many years. The roads have become busier and more houses have appeared, but the countryside remains open to us to explore and enjoy on our bikes.

1

Watford, Cassiobury, and Chenies

21 miles

It isn't always easy to escape from a busy town, but this is a good way out of Watford (and getting out of Watford was why I started cycling in the first place!). This route covers a small patch of Hertfordshire snuggling up to Buckinghamshire. Yes, it is hilly, as it is squeezed between the valleys of the rivers Gade and Chess, but the scenery and the villages please the eye and there are innumerable good pubs for drinks and meals. Traffic is usually light, as the M25 and two other main roads carry most of it. Chenies Manor, strictly speaking, is in Buckinghamshire, but its historical associations with Henry VIII and its fascinating physic garden make it well worth a visit if you have time.

Map: OS Landranger 166 Luton & Hertford (GR 095965).

Starting point: Watford Metropolitan station, Marylebone, London to Watford line. There is a car park at the station and other car parks in Watford itself.

Refreshments: All the public houses mentioned in the text cater for meals, but particularly recommended are the Clarendon Arms at Chandler's Cross, the Windmill at Chipperfield and the Coffee Shop in the Garden Centre at Tower Hill.

The route: After an easy start, there is a climb up past the Grove from the canal, another up to Chenies and back across the River Chess up to Flaunden. Apart from these there is a brisk and narrow descent from Sarratt and a lot of smaller undulations in between. Low gears will make light of most of these, however, and the mile or so off-road is quite well surfaced, though the lane up to Chenies could do with some repairs!

From the station, where there is a small snack bar, **turn R** onto Cassiobury Park Avenue and at the next junction **turn L** onto Shepherds Road, signed 'Toilets', into Cassiobury Park. **Bear L** on the shared cycle path and follow it round to the right. (Unfortunately the straight through route is still No Cycling.) At the road cross over into The Gardens and at the next crossroads but one **turn L** onto Cassiobury Drive, then straight over the roundabout to the end of the road, following cycle-route signs towards Langleybury. Then take the shared footpath straight on to the next road and take the **second L turn**, Stanbury Avenue. Stay on the major road and pass through the barrier at the end to Grove Mill Lane, where **turn L** past

Sarratt, visited on the ride

the converted mill and uphill beside the grounds of The Grove, a historic house, now under major renovation and surrounded by a golf course.

Take the **next L**, to Chandler's Cross; the Clarendon Arms pub is on your right, where **turn R and L**, staying on the major road, over the motorway through Micklefield Green and **bear L** into Sarratt, with its long village green. After passing the Cricketers pub on your left, **bear L**, passing the post office stores, and **turn L** at the crossroads, descending the steep, narrow lane into Sarratt Bottom.

Turn R and at the next right bend **keep L** through the gate, signed 'Public Footpath Latimer 2', on a gravel drive to **turn L** to cross the river Chess on a footbridge. You will have to lift your bike over a low bar here! Follow the rough little lane uphill to reach the road proper near Chenies.

Turn left to look at the pretty green or visit Chenies Manor or either pub, the Bedford Arms or the Red Lion, then retrace you way downhill to a tricky **fork R (care)** at the bottom (no sign). Another steady climb brings you level with the aerials at Martin Top, then **keep L** into Flaunden.

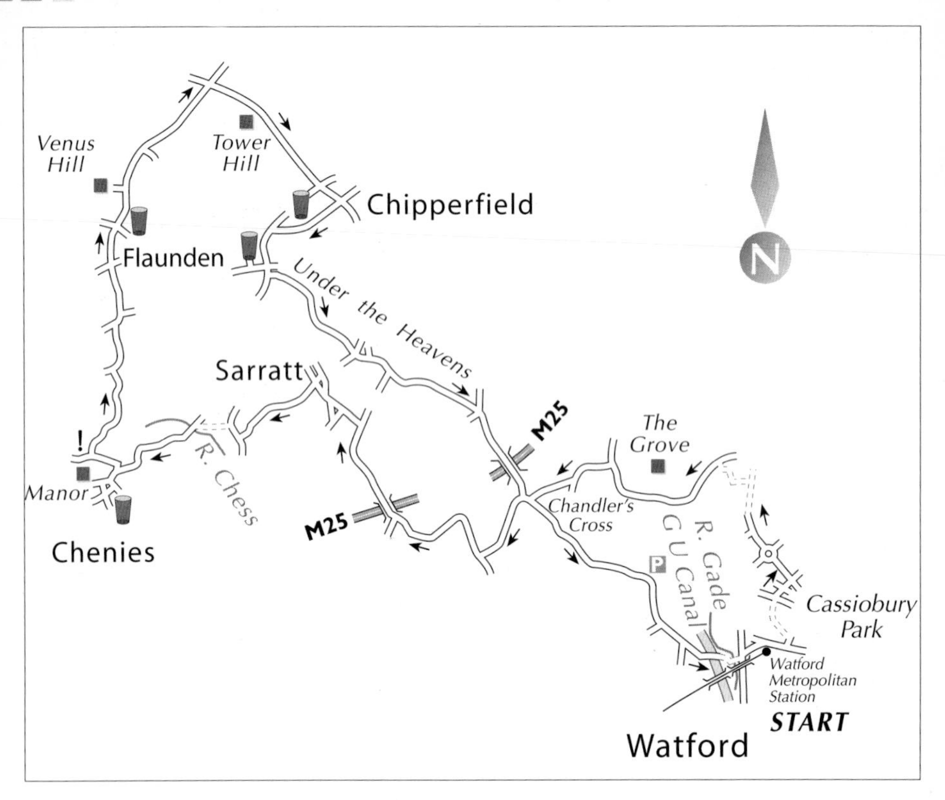

Keep straight on at the crossroads at Flaunden. The Green Dragon pub is off to the left and at Hogspit Bottom the Bird in Hand pub is on the right. Continue through Venus Hill to the next crossroads, where **turn R**, signed to Chipperfield. At Tower Hill, on your right is Wyevale Garden Centre for snacks and light meals; the pub on your left is the Boot. Go straight over the crossroads in the village to take the next **turn R** by the Common and the Two Brewers Hotel. Continue past the church on the left. Shortly on your right you pass the Windmill pub and descend Windmill Hill to **turn L** to Belsize, the Plough public house is on your right.

Keep L here and take the small road signed 'Plough Lane'. My local cycling club has known this little lane as 'Under the Heavens' for at least 80 years, though you won't find it called such on any map. Potter gently downhill to **bear R** at the end, up Toms Hill, then over the M25 and back into Chandler's Cross.

Bear L and immediately R down Rousebarn Lane, signed 'No Through Road', carefully avoiding the barriers halfway along. After

The village pub in Belsize

the housing begins, take the left fork, signed 'Gade Bank' and 'Weak Bridge', uphill past the golf club on the left and descend to cross the canal. Follow the track forward, keeping right at the fork. Continue along the edge of the wood to a footbridge on your left. Cross over the river Gade and **turn L** on the road, then **R** onto Swiss Avenue and **R** again onto Cassiobury Park Avenue to the station.

CASSIOBURY PARK

At one time Watford was the 'ford' at the bottom of the present High Street, while the area round the town hall was the hamlet of Cassio. At the time of the Restoration, the land was returned to the Capel family, who became Earls of Essex and built a new Cassiobury House. In 1800 the 5th Earl had it remodelled in the Gothic style, but in 1922, despite its luxurious interiors, it was demolished. With great forethought the Borough Council retained a large area of the grounds as a public park for Watford. Since town centre road widening which destroyed the old park entrance lodge, the only remnants of the former estate buildings are two other small lodges and part of the stables, which have been converted into a comfortable old people's home. The amazing carved staircase from the house is now in the Metropolitan Museum of Art in New York. The park has been used for a good many sporting activities, including both cyclo-cross and massed start cycle racing.

THE GROVE

The house was the home of the Earls of Clarendon from 1753 to 1935. The present house was built by Sir Robert Taylor in 1756, but has had various alterations since. It was used during the Second World War for various hush-hush activities and eventually became a training centre for the British Railways Board. It is now undergoing further alterations and may well become a most superior golf clubhouse.

2

Off-road round St Albans

10 miles

Because this route has a large proportion of off-road riding, it is best tackled after or during a dry spell, but there is nothing particularly difficult or technical involved. Two old great estates are crossed and it is particularly pleasing to feel you can cycle where the motorist may not go and to see some of the playgrounds of the wealthy. There are also opportunities to see fine examples of our ancient history from Roman and medieval times in St Albans and the more domestic memories of two preserved watermills.

Map: OS Landranger 166 Luton & Hertford (GR136073).

Starting point: Verulamium Museum car park on the west side of the city next to St Michael's church, close by the A4147 just south of its junction with the A5153, Verulam Road. If you arrive at St Albans main line station, turn right to the town centre, turn left and right again at the traffic lights close to the Abbey, then, keeping left, descend beautiful Fishpool Street (Kingsbury Watermill Museum on your left) and you will find the starting point on the left just after crossing the river Ver at the bottom of the hill. From St Albans Abbey station, cross the foot of Holywell Hill, turn right and then left, to walk across the park to the museum. There is no cycling in the park below the Abbey.

Refreshments: There is really only one pub on the route, at Harpenden Common, but there are many good picnic spots if you carry your own food with you and there are many places once you return to St Albans, not least the Abbey Refectory.

The route: Almost half of the route is off-road and stays fairly high as you are only crossing one main valley and the headwaters of the river Ver. I use a normal road bike for all these tracks, but the tyres are fairly wide and have plenty of tread. A mountain bike with some additional springing would, however, add to your comfort.

From the car park and perhaps after a visit to the museum (open Monday to Saturday 10 am to 5.30 pm, Sunday 2 pm to 5.30 pm), **turn L** and cross directly over the A4147 at the lights to the entrance to Gorhambury. The drive is a permissive bridleway and sensible cyclists are welcome. Follow the drive uphill, **bearing R** past the house's present-day entrance to the evocative ruins of Old Gorhambury

The ancient city of St Albans

mansion, worth more than a passing glance. Continue from here, **bearing L** downhill past a cottage, then **R** up the valley on a road that is initially unsurfaced. Pass below the junction of the M1 and the M10, then **turn R** along the A4147 with **care** for less than ½ mile, where **turn R (care)** along Westwick Row.

At the staggered crossroads **turn R** to the roundabout on the A414, where cross over with **great care.** Continue forward across the next roundabout, Green Lane, past the oil depot to the next roundabout, where **turn R** into Hog End Lane and under the M1. Take the next **turn L**, opposite a post box and past Old Jeromes, and **R** at the next T-junction. These narrow lanes, once so remote, are now just on the outskirts of Hemel Hempstead and its industrial presence, but make an excellent escape route.

Rapidly leaving the sound of traffic behind, descend to the old Watling Street, on the line of the Roman road to North Wales from Verulamium and London; cross with **care** and use the shared cyclepath to the **L**. At the next junction **turn R** and cross the two fords via the footbridges; only the very foolhardy attempt to ride through and we have seen wet feet on every occasion! Redbournbury watermill is on your left nearby,

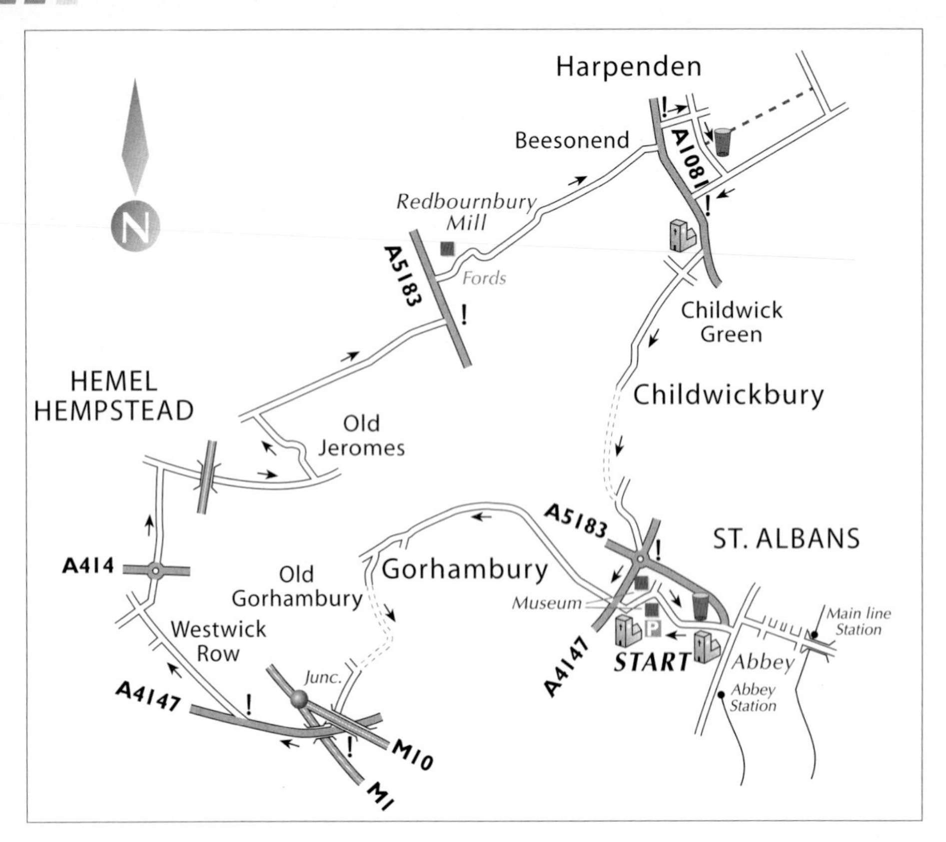

built in the 18th century and working regularly up to the 1950s. It has now been restored and produces organic stone-ground flour. It is open during bank holidays from Easter to August, 10 am to 5 pm, and serves teas on Sundays from April to the end of September.

A gentle climb from here takes you to Beesonend and the A1081. **Turn L** and **next R (care)** on Cross Lane, then **next R** at a crossroads alongside the golf course on East Common. On the left is the Three Horseshoes pub. Carry straight on to the T-junction, where **turn R**, then cross the A1081 **(care)** and **turn L** on the cyclepath to the big white gates of the bridleway entrance to Childwickbury estate in about ¼ mile.

Turn R through the gate and follow the bridleway signs through Childwick Green, a picturesque and beautifully kept 'village', once home to the estate workers of Childwickbury, latterly the home of the late Stanley Kubrick, the film director. The chapel of St Mary was built by Gilbert Scott in 1867. Keep left where the track bears right to

Redbournbury watermill

Shafford Farm and you will eventually reach the drive to the golf club at Batchwood Hall. Keep right to join the road, **turn R** and straight over the roundabout, then **turn L** at the traffic lights and **immediately right** to return to the Verulamium car park.

ST ALBANS

St Alban was a 3rd century Roman soldier, venerated as the first Christian martyr in Britain. He was beheaded for sheltering a fugitive Christian priest who had converted him. King Offa of Mercia founded a monastery on the site of St Alban's execution in AD 793, and later the magnificent Norman abbey rose on the site, much of its construction using Roman bricks from the nearby ruins of Verulamium. The town still contains a medieval clock tower dating from around 1412 and overhanging and half-timbered houses and shops. The Olde Fighting Cocks Inn beside the park was once thought to be the oldest inhabited house in England, but in fact was originally an octagonal pigeon house c.1400, re-erected here in 1600, where it became a centre for cock fighting in the 17th and 18th centuries until 1949, when the sport became illegal.

GORHAMBURY

The old house was once the home of Sir Francis Bacon, whose father, Sir Nicholas Bacon, built it between 1563 and 1568. Although it is now a ruin, replaced by a new and handsome mansion across the park, Queen Elizabeth I enjoyed staying here and was heard to say to Sir Nicholas, 'My Lord, your house is too little for you.' To which he replied, 'No, Madam, but 'tis your Highness has made me too great for my house!' Sir Francis Bacon is buried in St Michael's church close by the museum, with a famous life-size statue in the chancel.

3

Ashridge and Ivinghoe

25 miles

Hemel Hempstead, once a tiny market town at the junction of two river valleys, is now too large and busy for the cycle-tourist, so it is lucky there is such an easy escape route from the railway station into the Chiltern countryside. The route takes you through parkland and beechwoods to a superb viewpoint across the Vale of Aylesbury and returns along the canal. Look out for poetry on the wall of the railway tunnel, deer in the woodlands and the oriental shop-cum-café – some of the many gems to be visited on the way.

Maps: OS Landranger 165 Aylesbury & Leighton Buzzard and 166 Luton & Hertford (GR 042059).

Starting point: Hemel Hempstead and Boxmoor station on the Euston, London to Birmingham line. There is plenty of car parking beside the river in Hemel Hempstead itself, but the route to the station via the 'magic roundabout' is not recommended. It would be better to park discreetly beside the golf course on the B4505 Bovingdon road, 600 yards south-west of the traffic lights on the A4251. Return to the lights and cross over to join the route.

Refreshments: Recommended cafés are Sanuk Café in the garden centre at Little Heath, with its superb cakes and coffee and the scent of joss-sticks; Town Farm Tea Rooms, Aldbury, in the garden or under a low timbered roof, and the café in Waitrose, Berkhamsted. The Valiant Trooper Inn at Aldbury does an excellent lunch.

The route: Climbs are mainly gentle, but there are steepish pulls up to Little Heath and from Ivinghoe over to Aldbury. Some descents require care. Superb views and some very quiet riding reward the efforts. The first ½ mile of towpath after Aldbury is narrow and on grass, followed by a short stretch on road, then the towpath is semi-surfaced through Berkhamsted.

From the station, **turn L** onto the A4251, the old main road from the station; pass under the railway and the new A41 to the traffic lights. With **great care, turn R** into the gated road, look for unusual Belted Galloway cattle on your left, then pass under the bridges (interesting graffiti) and over the canal to **turn L** along Chaulden Lane. At the next T-junction **turn L** under the railway and **R** onto Pix Farm Lane, then **R** at the next T-junction uphill, passing some most desirable barn conversions and the oddly named Justa Farm. At Little Heath

Aldbury

look out for the Sanuk Café sign on the right at a crossroads.

Continue to the next T-junction and **turn L**, signed 'Potten End'. At the village green **turn R**, then go straight over the crossroads **(care)** and **L** onto Vicarage Road, signed for Frithsden. At the end, **a R** will bring a welcome descent with a glimpse of Gaddesden Place ahead, to **sweep L** at the bottom, signed for Frithsden, past the house with bulldogs on the gate (once home to a Crufts champion) and into the village, with its pretty pargeted Little Manor and the Alford Arms pub. A detour to the right in this hamlet will take you to Frithsden Vineyard (ring for details of open days well in advance, telephone: 01442 864632).

Following the valley gently uphill (sometimes uncommon longhorn cattle on the right) and **bearing R** at the next junction brings you into Ashridge Park, where cyclists go free, but motorists pay a toll. Passing the front of the magnificent, turreted house, now a college, the road descends (watch out for the traffic calming humps) and climbs again to Little Gaddesden. Straight over the crossroads takes you to the church to visit the Bridgwater tombs. **Turn L** at the crossroads, past a useful pub and a village shop, to Ringshall.

Turn L onto the B4506 in Ringshall and immediately **R** under the shady beeches of Ivinghoe Common. It is a gentle climb;

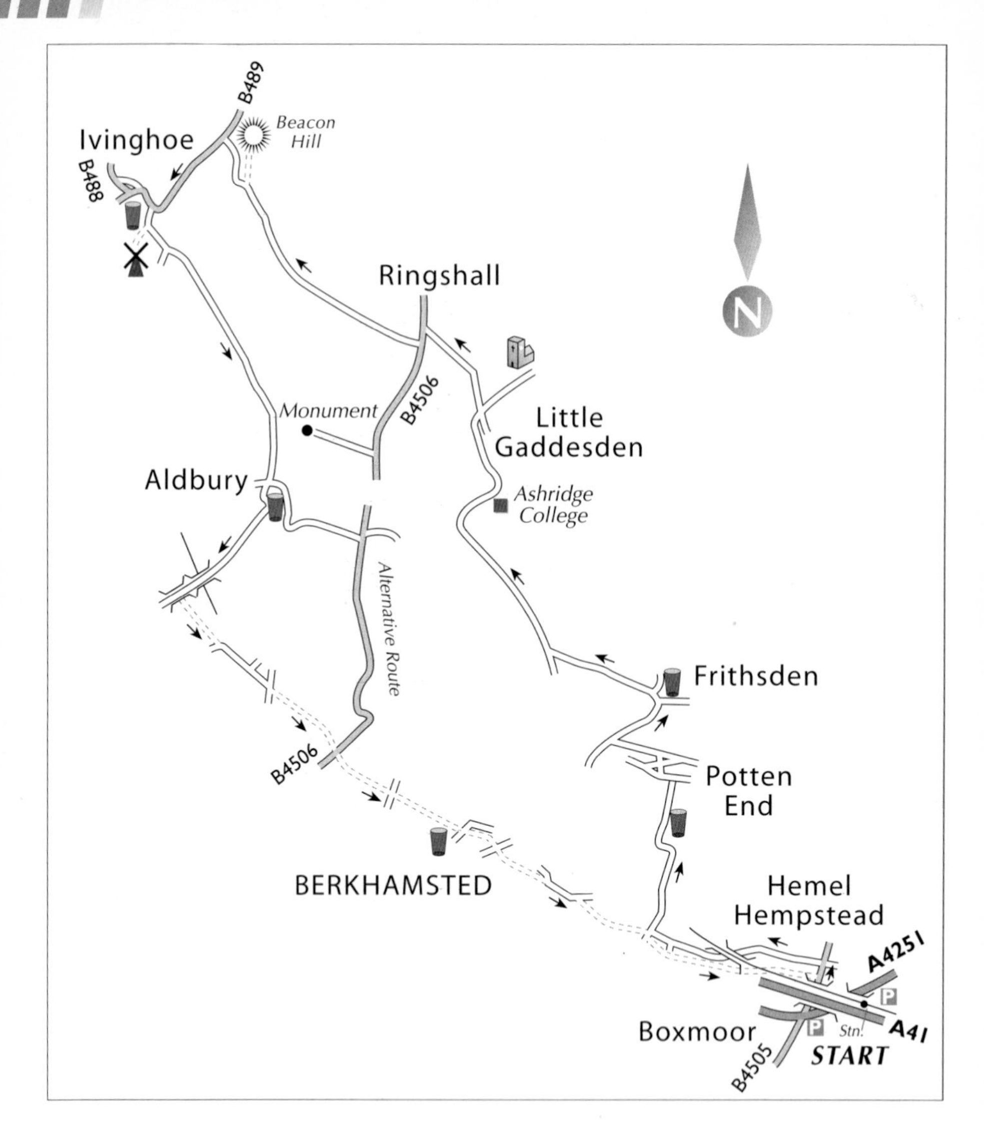

then, suddenly, the trees part and the views begin.

Ahead of you is Ivinghoe Beacon. On the sharp left-hand bend, park your bike nearby, locked up, of course, and walk to the top of the Beacon for the views and perhaps a display by model aircraft enthusiasts, who love this spot. Take your map with you, there is much to identify; on a good day you can see far into Oxfordshire, Bedfordshire and across to the Berkshire Downs. The big house you can see on the hill some four miles away is Mentmore Towers, built by Baron Meyer de Rothschild

The delightful village of Ivinghoe

and once the home of Lord Rosebery and some very fast horses! You are also not far from Cheddington of Great Train Robbery fame. To your right is the chalk figure of the Whipsnade lion.

Back to the bike, descend the hill with **care** and **turn L** onto the B489, which can be busy. It is worth turning right into Ivinghoe village. You can see, and sometimes visit, Ford End watermill, 500 yards along the B488 (opposite the Youth Hostel), open occasionally between Easter and September, 2.30 to 5.30 pm. Telephone 01582 600391 or 01296 661997. On the wall of the churchyard, by the Youth Hostel, there is a thatch hook for removing burning thatch. The church is also interesting and there are three pubs in the village, including Bernard Miles' Rose and Crown, if you are old enough to remember him on the radio.

Otherwise **turn L** and pass or visit Pitstone windmill (open June to August, Sundays 2.30 to 6 pm) and on the sharp right-bend carry straight on, unsigned, uphill and over to Aldbury, with its much photographed pond (said variously to contain a coach and four or a First World War tank), surrounded by picturesque houses.

After suitable refreshment at café, pub or shop, you have a choice of routes. For those who love the waterside, continue past the

Valiant Trooper to the canal, just after the railway bridge, **turn L** onto the towpath and follow it through Berkhamsted back to the bridge (No. 148) you crossed about a quarter of a mile from Hemel Hempstead railway station. The path is a bit rough, but only for the first ½ mile. The alternative is to **turn L** in Aldbury, climb Tom's Hill through the beechwoods to the B4506, where **turn R** and descend to the canal bridge at Northchurch, where **turn L** on the good towpath through Berkhamsted to Boxmoor. **Turn R** at bridge no. 148 and pass under bridges to traffic lights on the A4251, where **turn L** to the station or straight on to the car park.

MUNTJAC DEER

This animal is an accidental introduction, having escaped from private parkland, and is often seen wandering quietly on roadsides or on the edge of woods in the evening hours. It is usually solitary, though the single fawn accompanies its mother until well grown. As it is just the size of a large dog and has only tiny antlers, it can be mistaken for some other creature. The main problem with this immigrant is that it can devastate garden flowers and vegetables, but it is otherwise an interesting addition to local wildlife. Any other deer you may see, if you are lucky, will almost certainly be the herd of fallow deer in Ashridge Forest.

ASHRIDGE HOUSE

This originally dates from 1283 and Queen Elizabeth I was once held a virtual prisoner here between 1553 and 1556. The house is now a management college. The gardens, which owe their design to both 'Capability' Brown and Humphrey Repton, are open to the public on Saturday and Sunday afternoons between April and October. The family of the Egertons, the Earls and Dukes of Bridgwater, lived here until the third and last Duke, who was more interested in backing James Brindley in building canals than in looking after the property, allowed it to fall into disrepair. Many of the family are buried in Little Gaddesden church (a ½ mile detour from the route). There is also a monument by Sir Jeffrey Wyatville to 'The Canal Duke', erected in the park in 1832. To visit this you can follow the route to Ringshall, then turn left on the B4506 for about ¾ mile (**care**, it is a busy road), then turn right at a sign on a broad driveway leading from the house to the monument. It may be possible to ascend the tower, and a café opens at busy times.

4

The Nicky Way Railway Path and Redbourn

15 miles

This railway path was developed by St Albans District Council and Dacorum Borough Council. It has been open since 1985, making an almost secret rural escape route from Hemel Hempstead into the still beautiful wide-skies countryside remaining between the town and the M1. As with other such paths, do remember that it is used by pedestrians as well, so give plenty of warning, preferably with a bell. Housing and factory developments complicate the first part of the route, but are more than compensated for by the long quiet stretches under arching trees. The two crossings of the A5, however, must be taken with great care, as it can be very busy indeed, but the peace of the countryside gained by these few moments of traversing the rushing traffic could hardly be more of a contrast. Winding, undulating and narrow lanes meander along boundaries of huge fields and grassy commons, past farms and coppices, almost traffic free.

Map: OS Landranger 166 Luton & Hertford (GR 052082).

Starting Point: Hemel Hempstead 'Park and Ride' in Gadebridge Road off the A4146 to Leighton Buzzard.

Refreshments: There are plenty of pubs and restaurants in Redbourn, but recommended is the friendly little Copper Kettle bakery at the northern end of the High Street for filled rolls, tea and soft drinks served until 2 pm. Also there is a choice of two pubs (the Three Blackbirds does food) and a village store at Flamstead.

The Route: Four miles of the route are off-road. The generally smooth gravel surface of the Nicky Way rail path makes for easy riding, and the climbs encountered are easy for a cyclist, not so easy for an engine. After Redbourn there are some long gentle climbs and before Flamstead the Chequers Hill is sharp but short. Low gears and fat tyres will make this an easy trip.

Ride through the car park towards the town and **turn L** onto the cyclepath. **Turn R** at the junction to the roundabout at the beginning of Hemel Hempstead Old Town, **turn L** and immediately **R (great care)** into Alexandra Road. At the end **turn L** into Midland Road and **turn L** into the entrance to the Nicky Way beside the car park of the Midland Hotel.

Flamstead

Take the path by the right-hand fence, not the old railway track. This path shortly passes along the edge of parkland, then **turns L** up steps with a 'wheeling path' beside them onto the line proper. Follow until the path swings away from the line and cross the A4147, with care. Continue on a new path to the Eastman Way Industrial Area road, where **turn L** to next **turn L** (by a sign for Flamingo) and rejoin the railway track on the right of the next right-hand bend. Under the M1 bridge it is very dark, so beware of big stones, then follow Route 57 signs to cross the B487, with care. To catch you napping, hidden round a corner and with awkward barriers, is the crossing of Chequers Lane. **A L** and **R** will take you into Redbourn.

It is worth continuing on Route 57 (not up the steps) to the bridges over the River Ver and the old A5, which is Redbourn High Street. On the left is an opening into a mini park on the site of the old station yard, with an information board about the railway and a picnic site. Continue along the line to the access point by a roundabout and **turn L** into Redbourn. The High Street shops will be on your left.

Leave Redbourn north-westwards on the High Street, then Dunstable

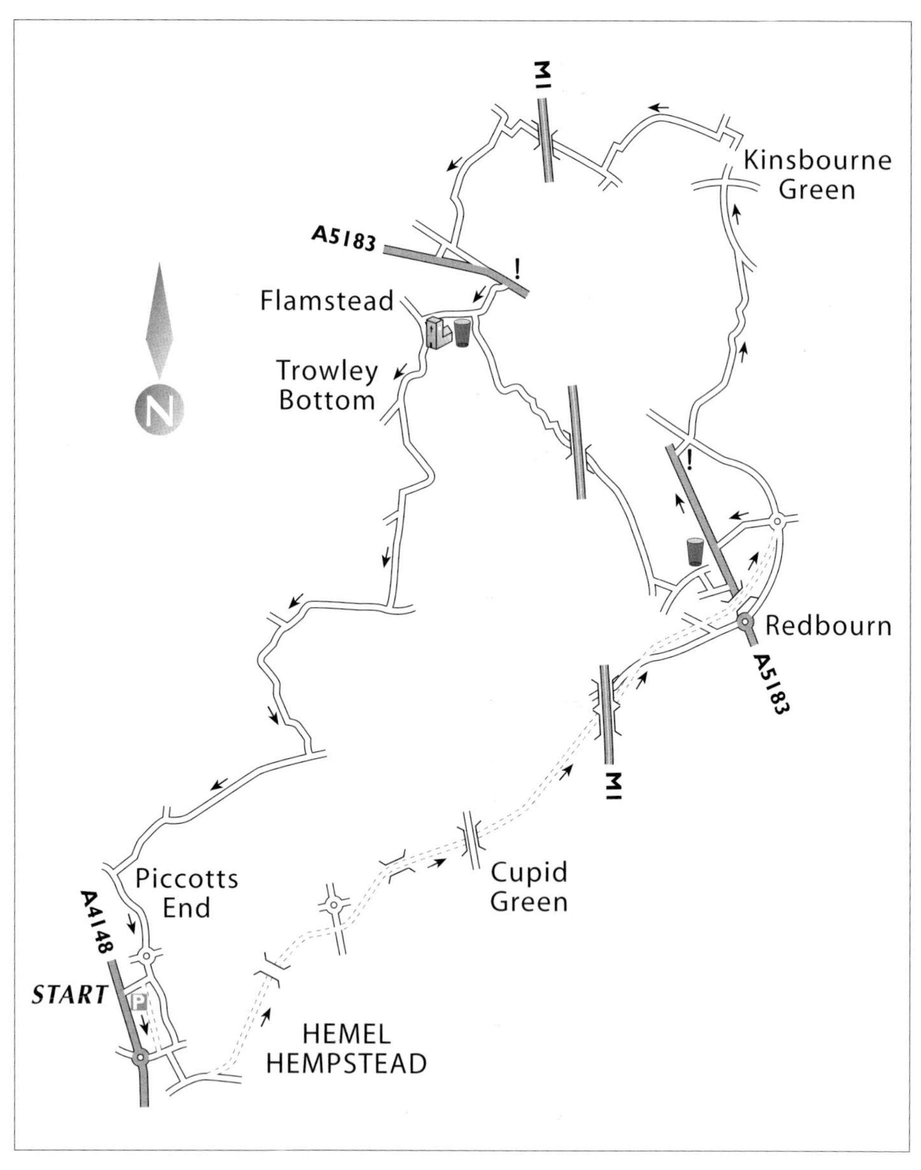

Road, to **turn R** at Luton Lane. Cross the A5* (**great care**, be prepared to cross on foot) and continue towards Kinsbourne Green. At a crossroads go straight on, signed Luton, on a right bend **turn L** and at the next T-junction **turn R** onto Coles Lane. At the next T-junction **turn L** onto Chad Lane, then **turn L** at the foot of the hill to cross the A5 (**great care**) up Chequers Hill towards Flamstead.

(*To avoid the busy A5 crossing, continue down the High Street to **turn R**, passing the broad common, and fork right, signed 'Flamstead', to rejoin the main route at the top of Chequers Hill, where **turn L**. This shortens the route by some 2½ miles.)

Climb the hill and **turn L** past the church, descend towards Trowley Bottom, **go L** down White Hill and **L** again at Trowley Bottom. Just after the de-restriction sign **turn L** past Greenland Farm and **R** past Stags End, then **L** again at Corner Farm, signed 'Cupid Green'. At the next T-junction **turn R** onto a narrow and unfenced lane, climb a little more, then descend to Piccotts End. **Turn L** past a fine converted watermill, half-timbered Piccotts End Farm and some pretty cottages.

Go straight on at the roundabout **(care)** at the end of the village, then take the next **R** into Gadebridge Lane and the car park is on your left.

THE NICKY WAY

Approximately 8¾ miles long, this footpath and cycleway is the former railway line known as the Nicky Line, which ran between Hemel Hempstead, Redbourn and Harpenden, a branch of the London North Western Railway, opened in 1877. It was built to link the straw plait trade in Hemel Hempstead to the hat makers of Luton. Apart from its main stations there were also a number of halts and sidings, of which nothing now remains. It was used to transport both local passengers and commuters to London, but numbers declined. A Ro-Railer vehicle, which could be used on road or rails, was used on the line experimentally in the early 1930s for a short period. The last passenger train ran in 1947. Commercial traffic was also on the decline, but for a brief revival when new industrial areas were developed around Hemel Hempstead. In 1968 what was left of the line was sold to the Hemelite Company to transport power station ash to their works in Cupid Green to make building blocks, but by 1979 traffic ceased and the line closed. The land was purchased in the 1980s by St Albans District Council, and Dacorum Borough Council, who added signage, surfacing and access points to make an excellent route for pedestrians and cyclists. A leaflet is available from information offices and the Countryside Management Service. Telephone: 01727 848168.

REDBOURN

Its name means 'reedy stream' and its early settlers included members of the Catuvellauni tribe displaced by the Roman settlement at St Albans. Its High Street is part of Roman Watling Street, later the busiest road in the country until the M1 was opened; it is now, thankfully, bypassed. St Amphibalus, the priest hidden by St Alban, was martyred on the common, and Redbourn Priory was dedicated to him. St Mary's church, with its beautiful rood screen, dates from Norman times. Other historical buildings include coaching inns and an old workhouse, rebuilt in 1790. Redbourn was also the home of the first ever cricket club, established in 1666, the year of the Great Fire of London.

5

Berkhamsted and Whipsnade

21 or 22½ miles

From busy Berkhamsted escape into the quiet lanes to visit the world famous Whipsnade Wild Animal Park, or at least look through the fence at bison, penguins and wallabies; but don't forget to explore Berkhamsted Castle, a fine example of a motte and bailey. Once a major stronghold, it is now just picturesque remains, almost hidden among trees, at the start/finish of the ride. There are also a good many hills on the ride, but the views will reward you.

Maps: OS Landranger 165 Aylesbury & Leighton Buzzard and 166 Luton & Hertford (GR 992081).

Starting Point: Berkhamsted station on the Euston, London to Birmingham line. You may be able to park in the nearby castle car parking space. There is also some free car parking at the top of the first hill, on the left at the war memorial.

Refreshments: A bit sparse on this route, but there are plenty of places in Berkhamsted itself. Recommended are the cafeteria in Waitrose supermarket (good cakes and a choice of coffee) and the Way In café, reached from the back of the supermarket car park. In Studham the Red Lion pub does a good lunch and there is a café in Whipsnade Zoo. It is probably a good idea to carry extra rations.

The route: This is quite long and noticeably hilly. Most hills are long and gradual but at Frithsden and Nettleden they are short but very steep. The descent to Great Gaddesden is rough (the only off-road on the route) and requires care, while Bison Hill is well surfaced and gives wonderful views. An extension of approximately 1½ miles is given, which cuts out a section of main road.

Follow Brownlow Road on the west side of the castle, bearing right to a T-junction, where **turn L** uphill. At the T-junction by the war memorial **turn R**. At the next junction **turn L** to descend the hill and at the bottom, by the house with the bulldogs on the gate, **turn L**, signed 'Frithsden'.

Turn R beside the village pub, the Alford Arms, up the hill beside Frithsden Vineyard and descend on a rough road to Nettleden. At the T-junction **turn R and L**, up another hill, over to Great Gaddesden. The attractive entrance to the church of St John the Baptist lies on the left; in the church are a good many memorials to the

The impressive Tree Cathedral at Whipsnade

Halsey family who lived in Gaddesden Place across the valley. On the 15th-century tower are some fearsome gargoyles and there are traces of Roman bricks in the fabric. The name of the village may come from 'Goat's Valley' and the river Gade rises not far away.

Cross the A4146 (**care**) and climb again to Gaddesden Row, where **turn L** to Jockey End. From here is an almost level road through to Clement's End, signed to Studham. The Red Lion is facing you by the crossroads in Studham. Go straight on through the village, and a steady climb past another pub and the village shop brings you to Whipsnade Heath. At the crossroads **turn L** onto the B4540 to Whipsnade.

On the right of the common is the track to the Tree Cathedral, a National Trust property consisting of an arboretum and the ground plan of a huge church laid out in hedges of laurel. It is a peaceful spot, ideal for a picnic, and in the autumn the colours of oak, ash and beech, maple, chestnut and cherry, backed by dark firs, make glorious riot. If you carry on along the road, you will shortly come to the gates of the Whipsnade Wild Animal Park. This is a place where you really need a whole day for a visit, but if you think you have enough time, it is open from 10 am to 5 pm in summer and 10 am to 4 pm in winter. Bicycles must be locked up in the car park opposite.

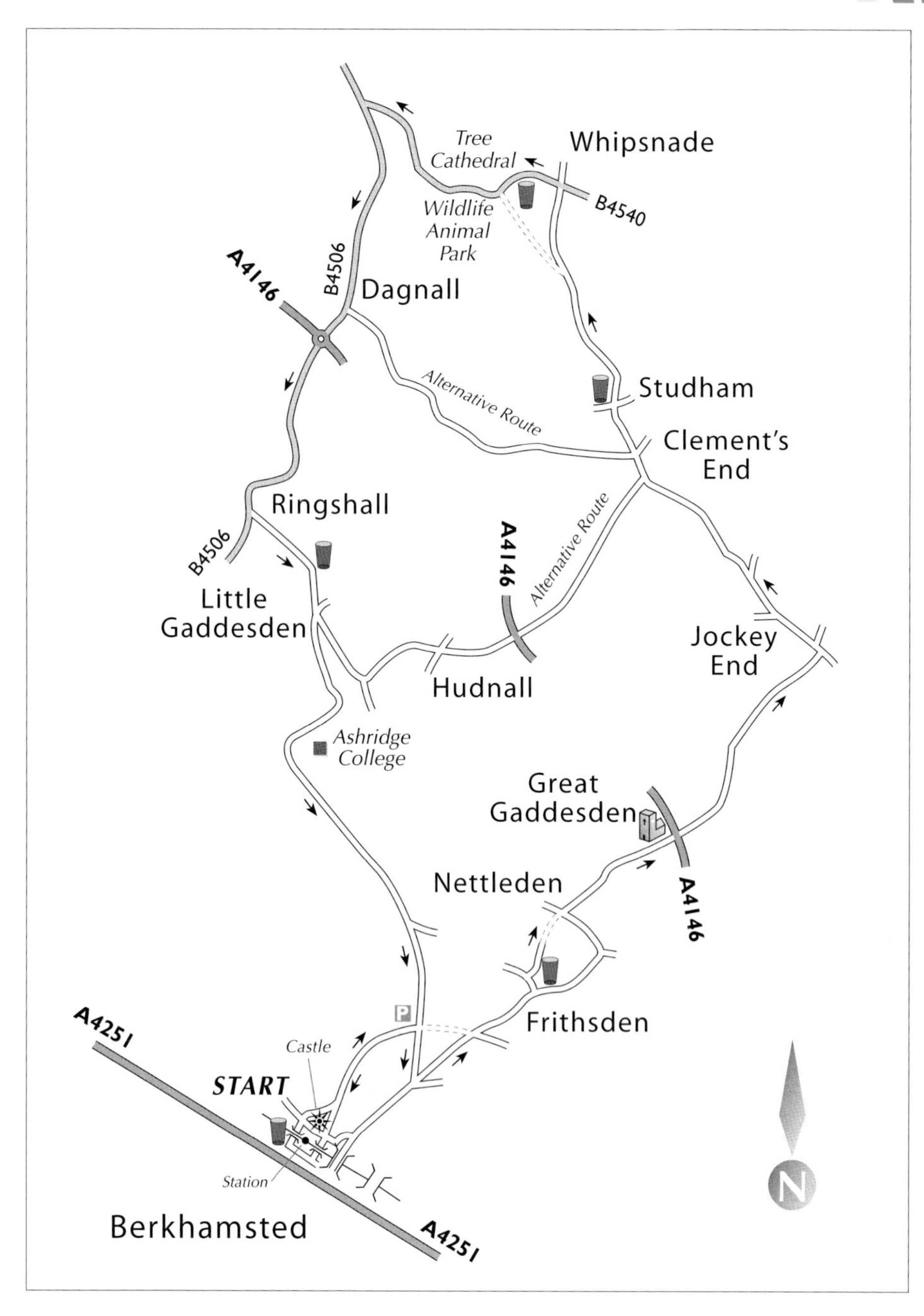
Tree
Cathedral
Whipsnade
B4540
Wildlife
Animal
Park
A4146
B4506
Dagnall
Alternative Route
Studham
Clement's
End
Ringshall
A4146
Alternative Route
B4506
Little
Gaddesden
Jockey
End
Hudnall
Ashridge
College
Great
Gaddesden
Nettleden
A4146
Frithsden
A4251
Castle
START
Station
Berkhamsted
A4251
N

Frithsden, visited near the start of the ride

From the zoo descend Bison Hill **(care)**. On the left at the top you may see penguins and bison, while wallabies graze at the feet of the chalk lion carved on the hillside. The views across the Vale of Aylesbury are magnificent. At the T-junction **turn L** onto the B4506 to Dagnall.

(To avoid further main-road riding **turn L** in Dagnall village and climb to Clement's End, **turn R** on Clement's End Road and **R** again to descend Pedley Hill, to the A4146. Cross **(care)** and climb again to Hudnall and Little Gaddesden, where **turn R** to rejoin the route, **turning L** at the entrance to Ashridge Park by the war memorial seat – this adds about 1½ miles.)

Continue straight through Dagnall and cross the A4146 at the roundabout to climb to Ringshall, where **turn L** to Little Gaddesden. Oddly enough, this village is much larger than its 'Great' neighbour! There are some very fine 15th- and 16th-century houses on the right of the long village green.

Opposite Church Road **turn R** into Ashridge Park and follow the road through the park (beware sleeping policemen), past the house. Keep straight on at the next junction, then in a sudden dip by the war memorial and a car park **turn R** to descend to Berkhamsted Castle and **turn R** before the railway bridge to the station.

The ruins of Berkhamsted Castle

BERKHAMSTED CASTLE

This English Heritage site, though now just a picturesque ruin, has a long and interesting history. It was a favoured residence of several English monarchs and Berkhamsted saw the Saxons surrender in 1066. The castle was built as a motte and bailey in 1086 by Earl Mortain and was restored in 1104. Henry I held court here in 1123. In 1155 Thomas Becket was granted the castle and spent large sums on the keep and walls; those we can still see. It was also held by Prince, later King, John and Edward, the Black Prince, who spent his honeymoon here with Joan, the Fair Maid of Kent. In 1389, Geoffrey Chaucer, the poet, was appointed Clerk of the Works and finally Edward IV granted the castle to his mother, Cicely, Duchess of York. After her death in 1495 it fell into decay. In 1582, Sir Edward Carey, Keeper of the Jewels to Queen Elizabeth I, was granted the manor of Berkhamsted and used much of the stonework of the castle to build a mansion at Berkhamsted Place. The present warden of the castle has spent a number of years researching its history and is prepared to deliver a two-hour lecture to groups.

WHIPSNADE WILD ANIMAL PARK

Whipsnade is part of the Zoological Society of London, whose key role is the worldwide conservation of animals and their habitats. The zoo-based animal management and captive breeding programmes here and at Regent's Park help to make a vital difference in saving species from extinction. It is possible to walk or drive round the park or use a tour bus, but bicycles are not allowed. Wallabies, peacocks, marmosets and Chinese water deer roam freely and many other animals live in huge paddocks in family groups. There is a children's zoo and a playground and the little train runs in the afternoons. There are free flying bird shows and feeding time displays as well as talks and demonstrations. Telephone: 01582 872171 for further information and special offers.

6

Tring and its canals

13 miles

Tring is a busy little market town in a gap in the Chilterns that has been used as a through route since Roman times and beyond. Akeman Street, now the A41, and its bypass, the Grand Union Canal and the railway all use this gap in the chalk hills, created by the waters of an ancient glacial lake overflowing. The route takes you on a loop above the town, because if you stay on the flat there are no views! Later there is plenty of scope for bird watching as you pass the reservoirs that feed the three local canals, and the return along the towpath demonstrates the work of the navvies who built the cutting by hand.

Map: OS Landranger 165 Aylesbury & Leighton Buzzard (GR 925114).

Starting point: Tring town free carpark (shops, cafés and toilets nearby) or, alternatively, start at Tring station on the Euston, London to Birmingham line.

Refreshments: A favourite for a snack is the Museum Café in Akeman Street, Tring, while there are many possible lunch stops, particularly the Half Moon pub at Wilstone, or, in Marsworth, the Red Lion, near the church, and the Bluebell Tearooms, by the canal.

The route: One testing hill, otherwise this is a flat, easy route with a stretch of gravelled bridleway through the park and a well surfaced canal towpath at the end.

From the car park in the centre of Tring near the handsome church, **turn L. Turn R** at the roundabout and take the next **turn L** onto Station Road (cyclepath available), to **turn R (care)** just before the canal bridge onto Beggars Lane.

If starting from the station, **turn L**, cross the canal and immediately **turn L** onto Beggars Lane.

Continue to the end of the lane, where **turn R** to cross the A4251 into Hemp Lane. Climb over the A41 bridge and up the hill to Wigginton, a village with a view across to Ashridge Park and beyond. At the fork **bear R**; at the crossroads go straight on (Vicarage Road, then Fox Road) for about ½ mile to the crossing point of the Ridgeway Path. Here **turn L** onto a gravel drive and into a woodland path in Tring Park. You may prefer to walk this short stretch. In about 100 yards **turn L** onto a drive which is a permissive bridleway

Marsworth church

with wonderful views of the mansion below and across to Ivinghoe Beacon. There is also an obelisk in memory of Nell Gwynne, who apparently stayed with Charles II at the original Tring Manor. It is also interesting to imagine Walter Rothschild driving his little carriage drawn by two zebras through the park.

Where the track meets the road, **turn R** downhill; pass under the A41 to **turn R** and immediately **L**. On your right is the Walter Rothschild Zoological Museum (entry free, open Monday to Saturday 10 am to 5 pm, Sunday 2 pm to 5 pm) and the Museum Café.

Continue down Akeman Street. Go straight over the crossroads in the town centre and the next crossroads (B488), towards Little Tring. Pause to admire the new bridge over the soon-to-be-refurbished Wendover Canal arm. In the distance you can see the towers of another Rothschild mansion at Mentmore. A brisk down and up and a **fork L** takes you to the B4089, where go straight on and **next R** to Wilstone. If you enjoy looking at water or birds, take a few moments to pause before turning and climb up the bank of Wilstone Reservoir on your left. There are usually many ducks, swans and grebes to be seen. In Wilstone are the Half Moon pub and a village store.

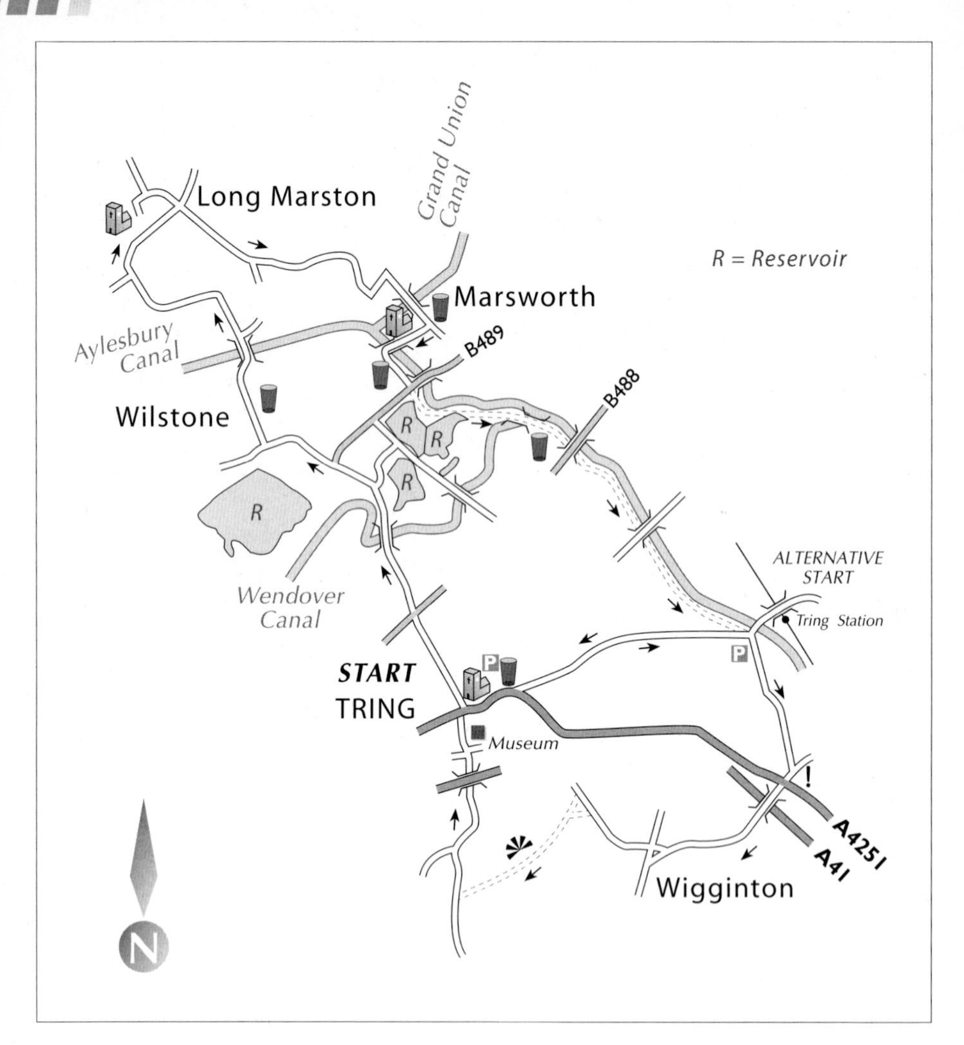

At the end of the village climb over the Aylesbury arm of the canal at a little humpback bridge, then **turn L** on the right-hand bend for the narrow lane to Astrope, passing the oddly named cottage, Dover Castle. **Bear R** on Astrope Lane to Long Marston. There is an interesting fragment of the old church, with gravestones mostly of children, if you turn left at the crossroads and left again onto Chapel Lane (pub and restaurant close by). Otherwise **turn R** at the crossroads (Queens Head pub – English and Hungarian food!) to Gubblecote, where **fork L** onto Lukes Lane. You will pass the remains of the old Second World War airfield and a tiny memorial on the left to the US 8th Army Airforce. After another big canal bridge comes Marsworth. After the

The view over Tring

Red Lion pub, on the left **turn R** past the handsome church with its old wooden tomb markers on Watery Lane, to cross over two more canal bridges by the junction of the Grand Union Canal with the Aylesbury arm. At the end **turn L** onto the B489 and **immediately R** before the traffic lights **(care)** into the canalside car park, where there are the Bluebell Tearooms and a choice of two pubs. Continue through the car park onto a wide path between Startops End reservoirs and the canal, then follow the towpath up the flight of locks to Bulbourne (and another pub, famous for its curries), under the B488, and continue through the Tring cutting to the second bridge, where climb up to the road. **Turn L** for Tring station or **R** back to Tring town car park.

TRING

With its Friday market and its interesting auction rooms, Tring is now a busy town. Its name derives from the Anglo-Saxon Treunge or Trehangr, which may mean a wooded slope. Close to the junction of Roman Akeman Street and the Bronze Age Icknield Way, it was nevertheless an isolated place until the coming of the canal and then the railway. Apart from the Natural History Museum, the church of Saints Peter and Paul is of interest, having a number of features, including gargoyles outside and curious corbels inside on the nave roof. There is also a fine monument to Sir William Gore, a

The canal at Marsworth

former Lord Mayor of London, who lived in Tring Park towards the end of the 17th century. The park is now owned by Dacorum Borough Council and is being restored as a public open space.

THE WALTER ROTHSCHILD ZOOLOGICAL MUSEUM

Imagine being given the land and money to build your very own museum for your birthday. This happened to Walter Rothschild when he was 21 years old, in 1889. His father was Nathaniel, the first Baron Rothschild, and he regarded his son's interest in nature as a harmless pastime. Nevertheless, by the time he died, in 1937, Lord Rothschild had gifted to the Trustees of the British Museum one of the greatest collections of natural history ever put together by one man. There was a condition that it remained a centre for zoological research and this continues under the auspices of the Natural History Museum. With its Victorian showcases, it retains its historic 'feel', but nevertheless is maintained with modern services and facilities. There are regularly-changed exhibitions and demonstrations, a shop, a café and two picnic areas.

7

A circuit from Harpenden

15 miles

Although Harpenden is considered to be a village by its inhabitants, it has grown to the size of a small town since the coming of the railway. Now one of its lines has become a cycle and walking path to Hemel Hempstead, but the main line station makes a good starting point for a circuit ride into the open, rolling countryside to the east and west. The views are wide and there is a great sense of spaciousness about this area. Clumps of trees and lone cottages break up the expanse of arable fields and the tiny lanes often hide between high hedges, resulting in surprising changes of scene at the next gap.

Map: OS Landranger 166 Luton & Hertford (GR 137142).

Starting point: Harpenden station on the King's Cross, London to Bedford line. Park on the west side of Harpenden's magnificent common and follow signs to the station.

Refreshments: There are plenty of shops and places to eat in Harpenden itself and the route passes a good many tempting public houses. Recommended is the Bright Star pub at Peters Green and there is a farm tea shop, the Higgletea Piggletea, open at weekends and in school holidays, near the route at Whitwell.

The route: The climbs are mainly gentle, winding and fairly long, as are the descents, of course. Take care not to be taken by surprise by gravel after wet weather.

From the station **turn R** onto the B652. Take the fifth **turn on the right**, Dalkieth Road, signed 'Crabtree Church', and **turn L** down Crabtree Lane, beside the school. At the bottom the Marquis of Granby pub offers food every day except Monday. Carry straight on over the footbridge over the river Lea.

Turn L and immediately **R** over the B653 onto Common Lane. After a short distance uphill, take the **right fork** to Mackerye End, a handsome 16th-century house, mentioned by Charles Lamb in his *Essays of Elia.* He used to stay in a nearby farmhouse, perhaps the one with lambs painted on its gate.

At a T-junction **turn R** to Marshalls Heath, where **go L.** At the next T-junction **turn R** to Gustard Wood, to the second crossroads, a junction with the B651, where **turn L** to Kimpton. (You might like to carry straight on instead, on Bullslough

Rothampstead Research Institute, Harpenden

Lane for 100 yards to the Cross Keys pub, then go back to the crossroads and turn right.)

At Kimpton **turn R** and immediately **L**. **Keep R** at the next fork and **fork R** again, signed 'The Holt', past Claggy Cottage. Across fields ahead there is a glimpse of St Paul's Waldenbury House, where Queen Elizabeth the Queen Mother spent much of her childhood, but the most noticeable landmark is the great white water-tower above Whitwell. **Turn L** at the next junction. If you need refreshment, turn right into Whitwell on the B651. In the High Street are two public houses and a post office shop, while the farm tea room is on the left, at the far end of the village.

At the bottom of the hill **turn L**, signed 'Lilley', and **next L**, Bendish Lane. Climb up to Bendish – no pub now, alas, but look out for some Gloucester Old Spot pigs on the right. Follow the lane through the village to Grove Farm, where **turn L** and **next R** to the edge of Breachwood Green. There are the remains of an old windmill here, but some way from our route, up a dead-end lane, a good ½ mile to the north. **Turn L** to Oxford Road, where **turn L** again. Along this lane is an excellent view of the end of the runway at Luton Airport, floodlit and busy with air traffic.

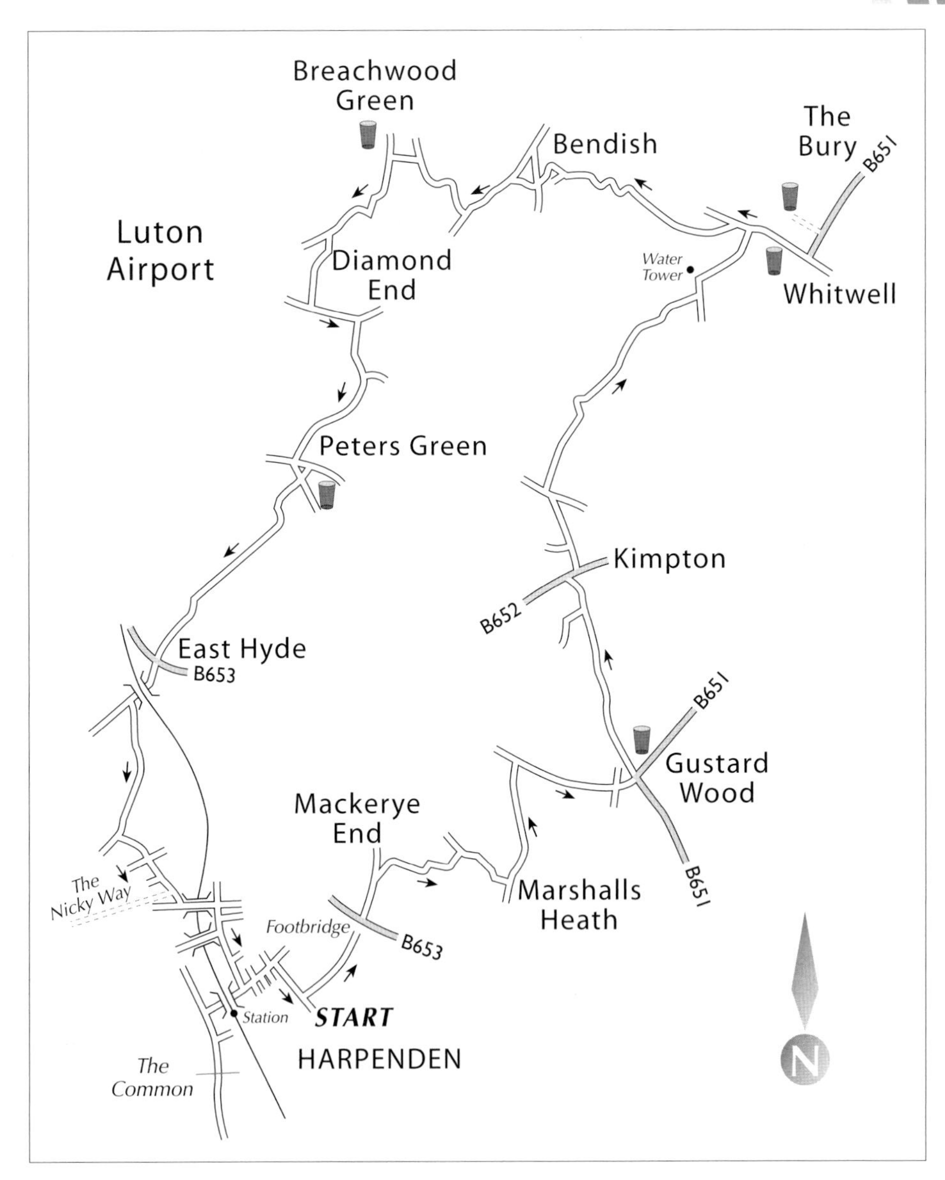

At a fork **turn L** through Diamond End, which used to house a surprisingly large collection of veteran bikes, now, unfortunately, dispersed. **Turn L** at the next T-junction and **next R** to Peters Green. The Bright Star pub is to your left.

Take the **R turn** opposite the pub, Hyde Lane, to drop to East Hyde. **Turn R** onto the B653, then **L** over the river Lea and under the railway and immediately **turn L** on Cooters End Lane. Then take the **first L**, Ambrose Lane, into Harpenden.

Claggy Cottage, passed on the ride

At the next T-junction **turn L, then R** onto Tennyson Road. At the next junction **turn L** onto Sun Lane over the railway, **turn R** onto Carlton Road and cross the B652 to Harpenden station. (Turn right downhill to reach the common.)

HARPENDEN

The approach to the town from St Albans along the old A6 coach road to the north-west is made memorable by the superb 238-acre common. Along the High Street there are more greens and many trees, which set off the handsome houses. It has also a notable town sign at the start of the built-up area. Amongst other architectural gems is the Old House; in the 16th century it was the Bull Inn and in the 16th and 18th centuries Harpenden Hall; it is now the council offices. For six years from 1864 the actress Ellen Terry lived at Fallows Green with her two children, before she returned to the stage and great successes. Harpenden is probably now best known for the Rothamsted Agricultural Research Centre, founded by Sir John Bennett Lawes of Rothamsted Manor.

CHARLES LAMB (1775–1834)

The English essayist was born in the Temple, London and spent the greater part of his life caring for his sister Mary. He was a friend of Coleridge and began his writing career in his twenties with a joint volume of poems, but his writings brought him neither reputation nor money for a good many years.

His first essay, *Recollections of the Old South Sea House*, was signed 'Elia' (the name of a foreigner with whom he had once worked) and his *Essays of Elia* were published in 1823. His works are composed in the form of personal confidences and his letters form some of the most fascinating correspondence in the English language.

8

Hitchin, Preston and Great Offley

20 miles

In the north of Hertfordshire, lurking between the built-up areas, lies an enclave of rural peace, its quiet interrupted only by the occasional plane taking off or landing at Luton. Although the hills are less high than those of the Buckinghamshire Chilterns, the scenery is similar. Rolling farmland is punctuated by hilltop beechwoods and every village has pretty cottages, a welcoming pub or an historic church or manor and sometimes all four. Take your time to appreciate them and, if you are fit enough, enjoy the hills too!

Map: OS Landranger 166 Luton & Hertford (GR 194297).

Starting point: Hitchin station on the King's Cross, London to Peterborough or Cambridge lines. There is a big public car park by the church. To join the route take the road opposite and turn left at the top and straight over the crossroads towards Great Wymondley.

Refreshments: There are no cafés on the route, but the Greyhound pub at St Ibbs comes at a good point in the ride, while the Plough pub at Ley Green is tempting too.

The route: From the start there is a short climb before leaving town, then the trend is generally uphill towards Preston and Offley. The route drops into Lilley Bottom, then up again to Preston, but plenty of downhill back to Hitchin. The scenery and pretty villages are your reward for effort and you may be comforted by the fact there are no really steep hills. Just make sure your low gears are working well.

From the station **turn R** and immediately **L** onto the B656. There is a cycle shop on the left, shortly. Take the next **turn L** at a roundabout, uphill on Highbury Road. At the top **turn L**, signed 'Great Wymondley', onto Wymondley Road. Continue downhill, under the railway and straight on at a mini-roundabout, out into the countryside and into Great Wymondley.

At the crossroads in the village **turn R**, signed 'Stevenage', with the Green Man pub on the right and the church down a side road to the right. Behind it, are the remains of a Norman motte and bailey, where a castle was built on the site of a Roman settlement. Further along on the right are the pretty Hornbeam Cottages. Continue to the roundabout and cross straight over the A602, signed

The hamlet of Ley Green

for Kidmore Green. At the next junction, by the Redcoats Farmhouse Restaurant and Hotel (perhaps too many stars for a cyclist?), **turn R**, signed 'St Ippolytts', keeping left at the second junction to drop down a narrow lane past a pretty lake on the right, to the junction with the B656 at St Ibbs. There can't be many places named after these two saints. Hyppolytus is the patron saint of horses, but his identity and the spelling of his name are in some doubt!

To your left is the Greyhound pub with a considerable choice of food and facilities, but the route **turns R** onto the B656 and **next L**, unsigned, beside the thatched St Ibbs Lodge. Continue to the next T-junction, where **turn L** onto the single track road (actually a little wider than the one you have just left). This is a really pretty mix of fields, woodland, hills and valleys. Go straight on where you join a major lane from Little Almshoe and climb a long steady hill, to **turn R** at the top (no sign) and into the village of Preston.

Here is a fine village green with a lovingly preserved wellhead and the Red Lion pub on your left. **Turn L**, signed 'King's Walden', then **go** straight over the crossroads, down and up again, to **fork R** (away from King's Walden). **Bear L** and **R** at Ley Green (or left

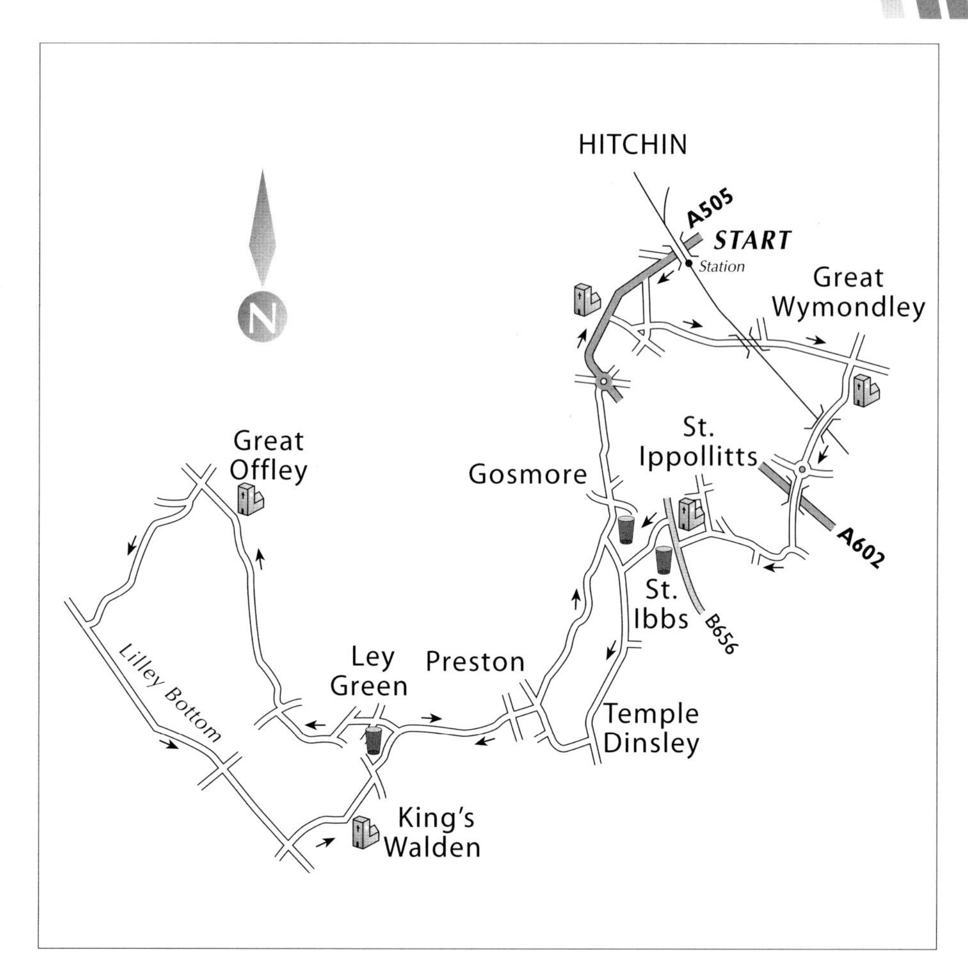

to the attractive Plough pub and retrace to the right turn). Then **turn L** to the T-junction, where **turn R** to the next T-junction and immediately **L** towards Great Offley. Go uphill on a wide drove type road, past a pond and into Great Offley with its unusual church, a jumble of architectural styles.

On the right is the mansion of Offley Place and there is the Green Man pub just before the crossroads. **Turn L** here, signed 'Lilley', where there is a village shop on the right. **Turn L** at a cycle route sign where the major road bears right and go down Luton White Hill to Lilley Bottom, where **turn L**, signed for King's Walden. Lilley Bottom is a typical Chiltern dry valley, though eventually a stream rises towards Whitwell, which is the source of the river Mimram. Go straight over the first crossroads, then uphill briefly and **turn L** at the next crossroads at the top. This lane is

Great Offley church

lined with clipped holly hedges and individual bushes all the way up to the sturdy little church on the right. There are two rare letter boxes in the village: one, made in Edward VII's reign, on the post office wall, the other, a George V, opposite the church. **Bear L** and **turn R**, following the sign to Preston. **Keep R** at the top of the hill into Preston on a short stretch of road you have done earlier in the opposite direction.

Back at the village green **bear L** towards Gosmore and the view opens out to the north-east towards Bedfordshire and Cambridgeshire. It is a good run downhill with just one sharp right hander and a little rise after. Then it is under the power lines, over a crossroads in Gosmore, past the Bull and the Bird in Hand pubs, both offering interesting menus, to a roundabout **(care)**, where take the **second exit**, the B656, towards the town centre. Go straight over the next mini-roundabout onto Queen Street. The car park is on the left by the church. Go straight on at the lights, signed 'Letchworth', and at the next mini-roundabout and the station is on your right before the next roundabout.

Preston

HITCHIN

Here is a town of ancient buildings and modern development, not always comfortable together. There are two Town Halls, one of 1840 and the other of 1901, but, for an insight into the history of the town, there is an amusing and instructive mural on Sainsburys' wall. There is nothing left of the 14th-century Carmelite priory, but the Baptist chapel of 1844 has a chair presented by John Bunyan, while the modernistic Friends' Meeting House was built in 1958. The church of St Mary beside the River Hiz is well worth a visit, both for its site and many items of interest inside, for which a guide book is needed to do it justice.

PRESTON

Here, there is a pretty village green with its wellhead and iron well mechanism. The church is a recent one, but there is a ruin of a much older one, Minsden Chapel, which dates from about the 14th century, a mile or so away. In Wain Wood, north of the village, is a dell in which John Bunyan used to preach. The mansion at nearby Temple Dinsley is built on the site of a community house of the Knights Templar, later the Knights Hospitallers. The present house dates from 1748, but was much altered by Lutyens in 1908. It is now a school and not open to the public.

9

Watton at Stone and Walkern

17 miles

Watton at Stone is 'next door' to Stevenage and, despite the prolific cycleways in the town, it seems better to start the ride in the countryside. The 'Stone' in the name may refer to blocks of the local Hertfordshire puddingstone, a remnant of flint conglomerate from the Ice Age, found in the village. The ride meanders through narrow lanes, through many hamlets and unspoilt villages with greens and ponds and spike-spired churches. There is a vast choice of pubs and picnic spots, a garden and a handsome windmill, yet none of it more than six miles from urban sprawl.

Map: OS Landranger 166 Luton & Hertford (GR 296192).

Starting Point: Watton at Stone station, on the King's Cross, London to Cambridge line. Parking may be found at the station. There is also a small space at the village end of the bridleway used on your return.

Refreshments: There are very many public houses on the route, all offering food and a great variety of architecture. Walkern probably offers most choice, but I rather liked the Rest and Welcome at Haultwick.

The route: There are no long hills to conquer, but the roads are rarely flat as you climb out of the valley of the River Beane and cross the arable land, occasionally dissected by its tributary streams. These lanes must indeed have been laid out by the 'rolling English drunkard'. There are plenty of wide views and open spaces for a picnic. The only main road is crossed just before the finish. Do please be careful there!

Turn L from the station and descend to the very handsome village pump at the bottom of the hill, where **turn L**. Go straight on at the mini-roundabout and **bear R** by the Waggon and Horses pub, signed 'Benington Lordship', over the River Beane and uphill over the bypass bridge. **Turn R** at the top of the hill onto High Elms Lane. Continue over Idle Hill to **turn L** at a T-junction through Burns Green, passing the Lordship pub, into Benington by the Bell on the charming village green opposite the Lordship.

Leave Benington on the Walkern/ Cottered road. On the right of a left-hand bend is the driveway to Walkern Hall. This is a good bridleway short cut to turn right to

Benington village

Clay End. If you prefer the road, continue downhill to the next T-junction and **turn R** to Walkern, going straight on at the junction with the B1037.

Walkern is a thriving village with three pubs – the White Lion, the Yew Tree, and the Robin Hood (Chinese food) – and a village shop. **Turn R** and join the B1037 (straight on) at the next junction, then continue through the village to Cromer. **Bear R** on the major road and at the top of the hill on the right you will find Cromer Windmill, a well preserved post mill, owned by English Heritage, open on Sundays, bank holidays and second and fourth Saturdays of the month, from mid-May to mid-September, 2.30 pm to 5 pm. Telephone: 01438 861662.

Turn R onto the narrow lane beside the mill to Ardeley, with its spiky Hertfordshire spire. **Bear L** at the Jolly Waggoner towards Moor Green, a handsome open common, with cottages dotted round and a pond beside a house called The Goose, perhaps a former pub. Then comes Wood End with another little green. Continue towards Great Munden on this rolling English road, but at Rush Green **turn R**, signed 'Dane End', and continue to Haultwick. On the left in Haultwick is a fine example of a half-timbered and pargeted cottage

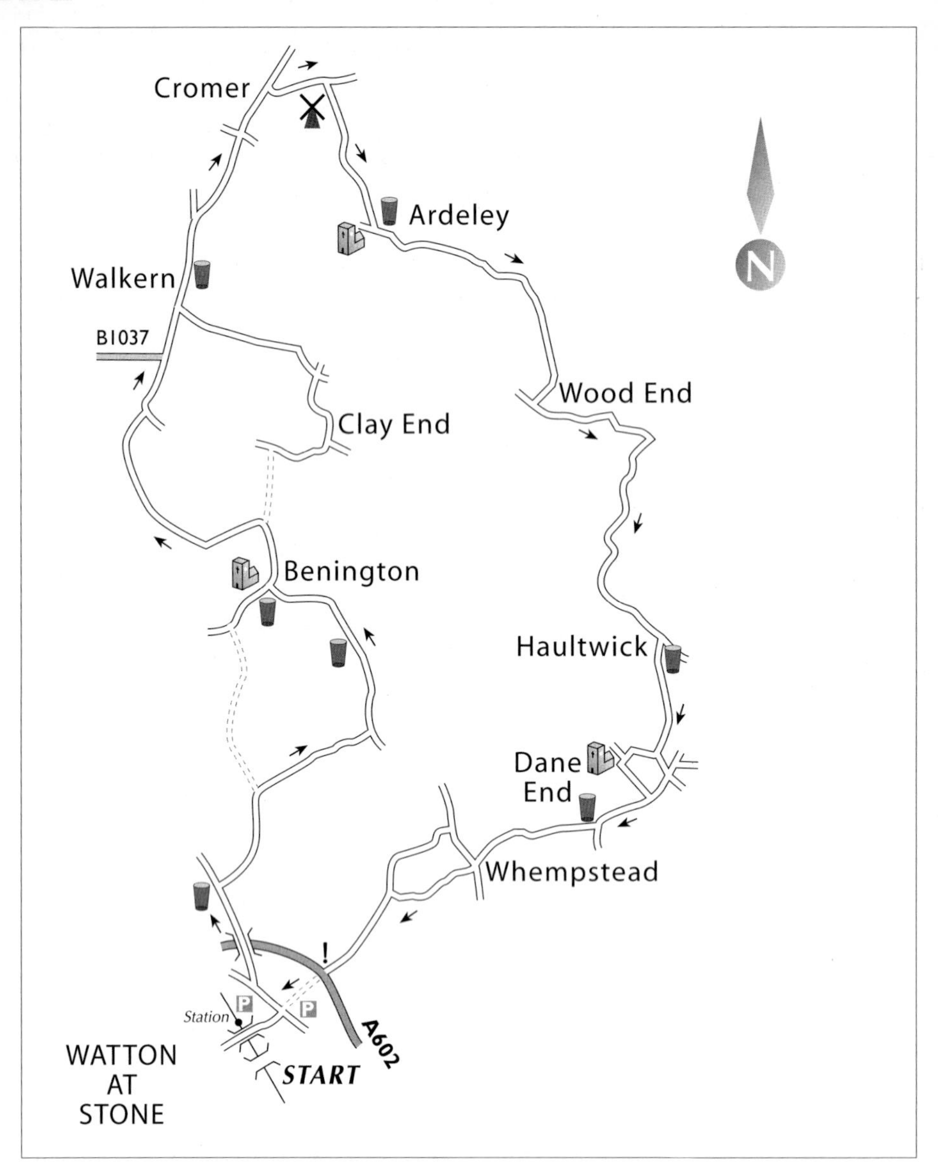

called The Bell, yet another 'pub with no beer'. However, just a little further on you will come to the Rest and Welcome, which has an interesting menu. Cinema enthusiasts may like to know that the Plough Inn at Great Munden (just off the route to the east) houses the organ from the Gaumont cinema in North Finchley. Occasional recitals are given.

Keep right and continue towards

Benington's handsome church

Dane End, but at the next junction **turn R** and follow the lane past Green End church, another needle spire. Continue on this lane, leaving the church on your right, and at the bottom of the hill **turn R** into Dane End, where you will find the Boot public house and restaurant and a little shop. **Turn R** in Dane End for Whempstead and go straight over at the crossroads, signed for Wotton at Stone. When the lane descends to the bypass, cross over the A602 **(great care)** and go through the gate onto the bridleway into the village. **Turn L** and **R** to return to the station.

BENINGTON LORDSHIP

Here is an almost unspoiled village with timbered cottages around a green, a pond, a manor house and a handsome church. Now an insignificant neighbour of Stevenage town, it was once a seat of the Saxon kings of Mercia. Later the family of the Benstedes, whose memorials rest in the church, lived in a castle once standing on the site of the manor house. Remnants of this castle were reconstructed in 1832 in the shape of a gatehouse to ornament a garden. The Lordship gardens, with their 19th-century folly, are famous for their snowdrop display and are open at Easter and on spring and summer bank holidays, on Sundays from 2 pm to 5 pm, Mondays 12 noon to 5 pm; also on three other weeks and an autumn weekend. Appointments can also be made. For information: telephone 01438 869668.

WALKERN

This village has a long history, being found in Domesday Book as Walchra and having many mills on the River Beane. The 17th-century Manor Farm has an octagonal dovecote beside the road and the church has Saxon remains in its nave and rood cross. Here there is also a rare 13th-century marble figure of a knight with his face hidden by his vizor. A less happy memory is that of Jane Wenham, the last person to be condemned to death for witchcraft in England, in 1711. Due to the good offices of the judge, she was granted the Queen's pardon and was given a cottage at Hertingfordbury for her protection, as she was afraid to return to Walkern. The Witchcraft Act of 1735 put an end to witch-hunting.

10

Welwyn, Knebworth and Ayot St Lawrence

17 miles

Despite the short distance between the 'old' new town of Welwyn Garden City and the new old town of Stevenage, there is, nevertheless, a stretch of wooded upland well worth exploration by bicycle. As you cross the B197 at Knebworth, remember that it was not so long ago that the Great North Road, carrying a thousand years of travelling history, was superseded by a motorway! Old Knebworth itself is better known for pop concerts than for the Bulwer-Lyttons' stately home. En route it is possible to visit Shaw's Corner, where that bearded cyclist/author penned many of his well known works. Finally, there is a taster of the cycleway through Sherrards Park into Welwyn Garden City for a glimpse of the local architecture and wide roads running down to the forty arches of Digswell viaduct.

Map: OS Landranger 166 Luton & Hertford (GR 247154).

Starting point: Welwyn North station on the King's Cross, London to Cambridge line. It is possible to return either from here or from Welwyn Garden City station on the same line. There is car parking below the Digswell viaduct, about ¼ mile south of the station, which is clearly signed from the nearby junction.

Refreshments: There is a snack bar at the station and a good many pubs and village shops on the route, particularly in Codicote.

The route: This is typical rolling Hertfordshire countryside and almost all on road. You will want a fairly low gear when you climb back to the railway station, as you have to gain the height of the impressive viaduct, but most hills are just steady climbs. There is one short stretch of off-road, using a signed cyclepath between Ayot St Peter and Welwyn Garden City. Do not be tempted by the nearby road to the south of this junction – it is one way, the wrong way! The cyclepath is downhill, but is not an ideal surface in wet weather, needing plenty of mudguard clearance and reasonably wide tyres.

Turn L from the station and follow the narrow lane to Harmer Green, where **turn L** and continue straight on through Burnham Green to the T-junction at Bull's Green. Here **turn L** to the crossroads and Datchworth Green (pub and village shop), then straight on past the Horns public house on Bramfield Road to **turn L** onto Bury Lane at

Ayot Green

the next T-junction and into Datchworth.

After the striking church with its tall spire, take the **second left turn** away from the sprawl of Stevenage and the next **turn R**. A pleasant downhill run takes you into Knebworth (pubs and shops). **Turn R** onto the B197, once the Great North Road, then **L** again to climb up from the River Mimram under the railway, **bearing R** and following the lane towards Old Knebworth. (There is no entrance to Knebworth House without going into Stevenage.)

Bear L past the Lytton Arms through Nup End, following the signs to Codicote. As you climb up again, the typical Hertfordshire needle spire on the church tower stands out. In the village you will find a restaurant as well as several pubs and shops. **Turn L** onto the B656, then take the **next R; keep L** at the fork into Codicote Bottom and cross the River Mimram again. At the T-junction **turn L** and **next R** up to Ayot St Lawrence on Lord Mead Lane. **Bear R** into the village passing the Brocket Arms Hotel and the ruins of the old church. Shaw's Corner is on the junction of the next right turn. It is open from 27th March to 3rd November from Wednesday to Sunday and bank holiday Mondays from 1 pm to 5 pm. To visit the classical 'new'

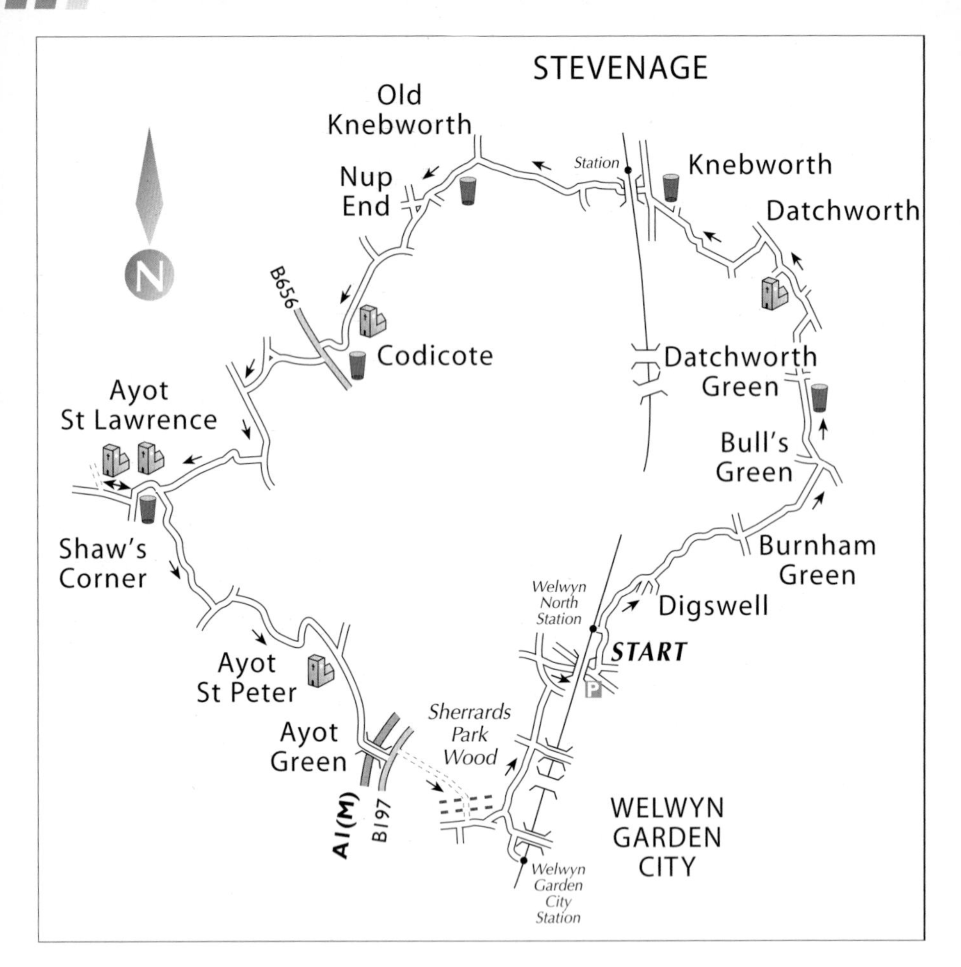

church, take this road and walk down the footpath on the right signed 'Church of St Lawrence'.

From Shaw's Corner retrace your route to the junction with Lord Mead Lane and continue along Hill Farm Lane past Hill Farm. At the next road **turn L** and **first R** to Ayot St Peter. Look right to see its unusual church clock, then go straight on to Ayot Green, a very pretty spot, but too close to the A1(M) for peace and quiet. Once over the bridge, **turn L** onto the B197 and immediately **go R** over the crossing onto Cycle route 12 through Sherrardspark, signed to the Great North Way. Keep straight on at all junctions (also follow a sign for Bridleway 18) to come out of the woods onto a residential road, where go straight over into Roundwood Drive. **Fork R** to pass between white railings on a continuation of the track, cross the Great North Way, a railway path, and come out on the road, where

turn L. Follow this road (ignore the right turn of Cycle route 12), and you come to a large green with a one-way system, near the centre of Welwyn Garden City. Follow round to the left passing Campus West and **turn L** into Digswell Road. Go straight over the roundabouts and descend to the A1000, where **turn L** and take the **next right (care)** into Digswell Park Road. This passes under the viaduct (car park on left); then **turn R** and immediately **L** to climb up and **turn L** to Welwyn North station.

If you decide to go home by train from Welwyn Garden City, from Campus West, with **care**, get into the right hand lane to continue round to the far side of the green, then **bear L** and you will see signs to the station pointing right. It is not very far, but rather busy!

KNEBWORTH HOUSE

If you could see it, the first landmark would be Knebworth House. You pass by the park, but the house hides in the trees. Here lived Edward Bulwer-Lytton, first Baron Lytton, from 1843 to 1873. He financed his extravagant lifestyle with a vast output of literary works and was well known as a wit and a dandy. He wrote many historical novels, such as *the Last Days of Pompeii*, plays and poetry, and edited at least one magazine. Although he is rarely read nowadays, his works span a wide literary period and are of considerable sociological interest.

AYOT ST LAWRENCE

Another literary giant is, of course, George Bernard Shaw, the Irish dramatist, who lived at Ayot St Lawrence from 1906 to 1950. His work is still performed and adapted and though he wrote a good many famous plays before coming to Hertfordshire, Shaw's Corner was the birthplace of *Pygmalion*, *St Joan* and *The Applecart*.

WELWYN GARDEN CITY

Welwyn Garden City was planned after the First World War and its chief architect was Louis de Soissons, whose Shredded Wheat factory became the epitome of the modern industrial building. The garden city movement was founded by Ebenezer Howard, and Welwyn and Letchworth were the prototypes of the self-contained community with both urban and rural amenities and green belts. In 1948 it was designated as a post-Second World War new town with Hatfield, but there was a proviso that space should remain between them and this has been achieved by parklands and lakes along the river Lea. The Digswell viaduct on its northern boundary carries the main line from King's Cross to Edinburgh. Six thousand navvies worked on it from 1848 to 1850 and it was built using some five million local bricks.

11

Bayford and Little Berkhamsted

12 miles

There are a number of pleasant country parks on the northern outskirts of London – Trent, Whitewebbs and Great Wood – but travel just a few miles further and you will be in wooded, rolling, rural surroundings that seem miles from the city. There are pretty villages and a mass of trails, mainly used by horses but available to the adventurous off-roader with a good map. The byways on this route, however, are comparatively tame, even after wet weather, but there are many horse riders using them too. Making it even more suitable for the family, on the way you pass the Paradise Wildlife Park, with rides, refreshments, playgrounds and events as well as the animals to enjoy.

Map: OS Landranger 166 Luton & Hertford (GR 315082).

Starting point: Bayford Station on the King's Cross, London to Cambridge line. Apart from the station it would be quite easy to park on the edge of Brickendon Green.

Refreshments: Snacks and Sam's Diner at Paradise Wildlife Park and a selection of pubs around the route. The Five Horseshoes pub at Little Berkhamsted has a good menu.

The route: There is just one appreciable hill on the route near the end and a small climb at the start and also out of Ponsbourne Park. The two stretches of off-road (totalling 2½ miles) are driveways with a fairly firm base.

From the station **turn L** uphill past the golf course and into Brickendon Green past the Farmer's Boy pub. **Turn R** by the green, signed 'Wormley'. **Keep L** at the next junction, then **R**, signed 'Broxbourne', then **R** again **(care)** signed to Epping Green. The Paradise Wildlife Park entrance is on your right in a short distance. It is open every day. For prices and further details telephone 01992 470490.

Continue past the park. There are several picnic areas on the left in Bencrofts Wood. Go straight on along White Stubbs Lane, signed to Epping Green. About two miles after the Wildlife Park and shortly after Bayford Boarding Kennels, **turn L** on the bridleway beside a lodge into Ponsbourne Park. Follow the major track, **keeping R** at the first junction, then round to the **L**. You then pass some cottages on the left and Windmill Farm Stables on

Stratton's Folly, Little Berkhamsted

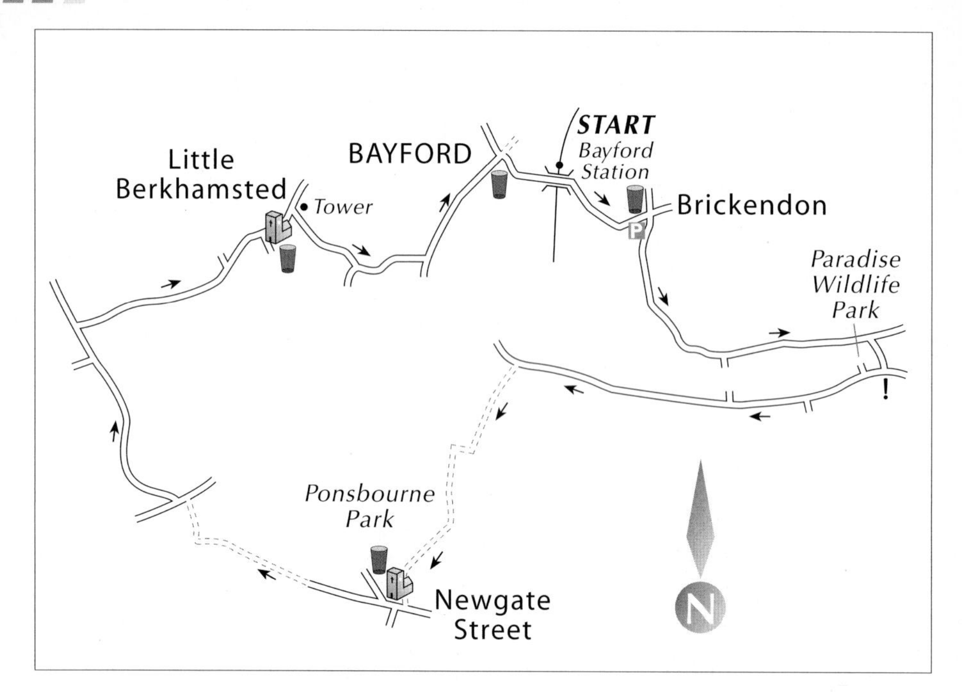

the right. The old walled garden on the right is now tennis courts and the track becomes surfaced. Drop down and up **with care** (sleeping policemen) to Northaw church. Ponsbourne Park House can be seen if you look back.

At the road **turn R** past the church and take the **second exit** at the mini-roundabout and almost immediately **turn L** into New Park Road by the restaurant; the Crown pub is on the right. Carry straight on when the road surface deteriorates and becomes a Road Used as Public Path. Pass New Park Farm on the left to emerge on the road at a staggered crossroads, where **turn L** and immediately **R** along Cucumber Lane, signed 'Essendon'. Take the next **turn R** (Berkhamsted Lane), down and up to Little Berkhamsted village, with its conspicuous war memorial and St Andrew's church, with a little wooden tower and shingled spire. Nearby is the Five Horseshoes pub and some pretty weather-boarded cottages.

Keep straight on, however, to look at the unique feature of the village, Stratton's Folly on Robin's Nest Hill. **Turn R** into Bucks Alley and drop down to the stream, a tributary of the river Lea, then comes the one real climb of the day. Take it slowly in a low gear and it's easy! At the top **turn L** into Bayford village and **R** after the Baker Arms pub and back to the station.

The delightful church at Little Berkhamsted

BAYFORD

Although the church is Victorian, built on the site of two earlier ones, its main claim to fame is in the churchyard – the grave of William Yarrell, 1784–1856, a notable naturalist and author of books on birds and fish, which were among the best of their time. He became treasurer and then vice president of the Linnæan Society. The great house of Bayfordbury was built by the Baker family in the 18th century and is now part of the University of Hertfordshire.

LITTLE BERKHAMSTED

For a small village, there are a surprising number of interesting past inhabitants. The striking tower of Stratton's Folly or Observatory was built by the retired Admiral John Stratton and was said to have served as a viewing platform so he could see shipping on the Thames, but this is not actually possible. More recently, Brian Johnstone, the cricket commentator, was born here. Perhaps the most famous local was Thomas Ken, born in 1637, who became chaplain to King Charles II and then Bishop of Bath and Wells. He wrote a number of well loved hymns, such as *Praise God from whom all blessings flow*, and he was one of the seven bishops who refused to read King James II's Declaration of Indulgence in 1688.

12

Sawbridgeworth and the Hadhams

25 miles

The Hadhams are strung along the valley of the river Ash and contain many beautiful examples of domestic architecture. Much Hadham appears to be the more successful of the two major settlements and includes Hadham Mill and Hadham Cross. Little Hadham with Hadham Ford and Church End is a smaller village at the junction of the valley road and Roman Stane Street (now the A120), which strides away across country to Colchester. Other hamlets on the route contain more pretty cottages and village greens, while Sawbridgeworth itself is a compact little town, worth more than just a second glance.

Map: OS Landranger 167 Chelmsford & Harlow (GR 490151).

Starting point: Sawbridgeworth station on the Liverpool Street, London to Cambridge line. There is free parking in the town near the church in Bell Street.

Refreshments: It would be easy to buy food in Sawbridgeworth before starting the ride, but there are a number of public houses on the route which cater and Great Hadham has a wide choice. I quite favour the Old Crown, but there is a tempting menu at the Nag's Head at Wellpond Green.

The route: This is gently rolling countryside – no big hills or fierce descents. Although the map shows a number of off-road possibilities, these should only be attempted in dry weather, as Hertfordshire mud has great clinging powers!

There is a short stretch of main road near Little Hadham, sometimes busy, but wide enough and with good visibility. A shortcut is described that will avoid the main road, however. This cuts out about 3 miles. The A1184, despite once being the A11, is now a quiet route for last ¾ mile or so back to town.

From the station, **turn R** and climb up into the town. There are plenty of shops and food outlets and a bike shop just on the left of the junction. Go straight over the pair of mini-roundabouts, signed 'Allen's Green', and follow the lane past the Three Horseshoes. After a pretty weather-boarded and thatched cottage and a good sized pond, **turn R**, signed 'Allen's Green'. Follow the major road into the village and round to the right past the Queens Head. Now you are heading towards Green Tye, across wide, hedge-free fields, perhaps a sign of modern farming, but the remnants of a pillbox suggest a defunct wartime airfield.

Much Hadham

Turn L into Green Tye across a pretty village green and past the Prince of Wales pub. At the next T-junction **turn L** into Perry Green, by the church of St Thomas, and pass the Hoops Inn. The road begins to turn from south to west and drops down beside a stream in a deep gully, passing a strange building on the right which may once have been lime kilns. The stream joins the River Ash at Hadham Mill and the route **turns R** onto the B1004 through Hadham Cross and Much Hadham, the latter with a post office shop, the Jolly Waggoners, the Old Crown and the Bull Inn offering food and drink, as well as teas in Hopkins Nursery just after the Bull. The village street also contains many fine examples of half-timbered and pargeted buildings.

Continue through Hadham Ford (usually dry) and Little Hadham to cross the A120 at the traffic lights and continue to Clapgate, where **turn L** at the almost hidden crossroads to Albury with the 13th-century church of St Mary on its hill. This contains several interesting features. Continue round to the left through Albury End and back to the main road, which is on the line of Roman Stane Street heading for Colchester. **Turn R (care)** onto the A120 for ¾ mile (this road can be busy) and **turn L** to Broken Green.

SHORT CUT: To avoid the main A120 and shorten the route by some

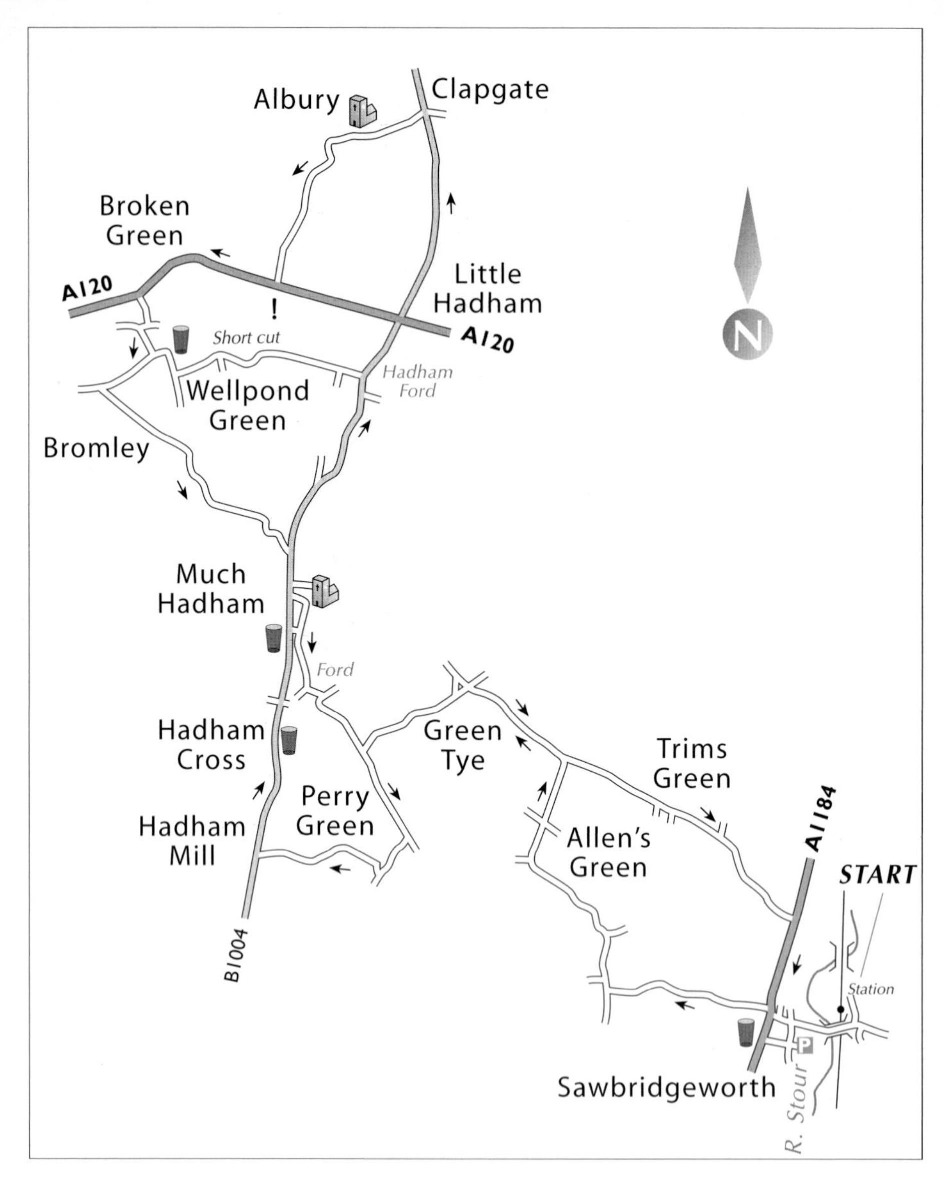

4 miles, **turn L** in Hadham Ford by a chapel and follow the lane through Westland Green to Wellpond Green, where you continue past the Nags Head pub to **turn L**, signed 'Much Hadham'.

A **right and left** bring you to Wellpond Green, where **turn R** at the Nag's Head pub. Take the **next L**, signed 'Much Hadham'. (A tempting byway route via Bromley crossing a ploughed field at one end cannot be recommended.)

The attractive village sign in Much Hadham

At the T-junction **turn R** into Much Hadham and take the **second turn L** past the church, following the lane to a ford on the left (shallow enough to try as a rule, but there is a footbridge if you need it). **Turn L** here and **R** at the top of the hill to the **next L** back through Green Tye. **Turn R** at the crossroads and keep straight on this road through Trims Green to the A1184, where **turn R (care)** for about ¾ mile on a not too busy road into Sawbridgeworth. **Turn L** at the pair of mini-roundabouts to return to the station or **next L** onto Bell Street for the car park.

SAWBRIDGEWORTH

Sabrixteworde is the name to be found in the Domesday Book, when the town had one mill. Nowadays there are still mill buildings by the river Stort, though many have retired from milling. In the town itself are some handsome buildings and the local history society have produced a pamphlet if you need more information. Houses in Bell Street and the 16th-century market house are particularly fine and Fair Green is worth a visit. The church was restored in the 19th century, partly by Gilbert Scott, but dates back to the 13th century.

MUCH HADHAM

According to Nikolaus Pevsner, the expert on English architecture, this is 'visually probably the most successful village in the county'. Over many centuries it has had palaces for the Bishops of London. The last palace is now converted into flats and stands north of the church. Edmund Tudor, the father of King Henry VII, was born here. The church has two heads made by Henry Moore, who once lived here, and parts of the building date back to the 13th century.

13
The Pelhams

29 or 38 miles

Take a sunny summer day, light breezes and an early start. This may look a long ride, but it is over easy country and there is much to see without leaving the saddle. The three Pelham villages each have their merits and date back to Norman times and, though the name of Stocking Pelham is thought to denote 'land covered in tree stumps', these days the rolling fields are full of productive crops. To the north of these villages are two other points of interest: the Second World War airfield at Nuthampstead, once a competitor for the 'honour' of becoming London's third airport, which has other interesting aeronautical history, and the village of Barley, on the border of Cambridgeshire, with its unusual inn sign.

Maps: OS Landranger 167 Chelmsford & Harlow and 154 Cambridge & Newmarket (GR 492209).

Starting point: Bishop's Stortford station on the Liverpool Street, London to Cambridge line. There is plenty of parking close by.

Refreshments: Furneux Pelham contains two recommended inns, the Star at the top of the village and the Brewery Tap at the bottom of the hill at Barley End. Otherwise there are a number of village pubs listed that cater, but few picnic places except perhaps churchyards and village greens.

The route: A basic route is given together with a 9-mile extension. Typical gently rolling countryside of the Hertfordshire/Essex borders is to be found for the whole of the combined route. There is one short, moderate climb into Furneux Pelham, but the rest is easy and you will be tempted to go just that bit further. On the extension there is just one more such ascent. The return journey from the most northerly point is chiefly in Essex, and has the advantage of a level or descending route following the River Stort.

From the station, **turn L**, move over to the right-hand lane, then follow the one-way system and the signs for Hertford A1250. At the first roundabout **turn R** onto the B1004, signed to Farnham. In almost a mile **turn L** into Farnham Road. After a short uphill section, you cross over the ring road on a bridge and you are out in the country!

Turn L at the next two road junctions signed to Albury and Upwick. Continue on this winding lane through Level's Green,

The thatched pub in Stocking Pelham

Walnuttree Green and Upwick Green to a T-junction, where **turn R** through Clapgate and Gravesend, passing the Catherine Wheel pub and **bearing L** towards Furneux Pelham.

To visit the pretty village with its 13th-century church and the recommended Star pub continue uphill and take the **second R**. **Turn R again** in the village to find the Brewery Tap (good value pensioners' meals) and continue the route. Follow the signs to **bear L** to Stocking Pelham, another village worth more than a second glance.

Turn left in Stocking Pelham by the Cock Inn, passing the little flinty church on its mound, and follow the winding lane towards Brent Pelham. After a right-hand bend, take the **next L** to **turn R** at the second 'Unsuitable for Motors' sign, just before it gets too rough to be pleasant. This quiet byway brings you to a pretty barn and duck pond, where you **turn L** into Brent Pelham. Keep right by the church, heading for Anstey and Meesden.

(At Brent Pelham you have a choice of routes. The longer trip will make your ride some 38 miles long, but reaches one of the most northerly Hertfordshire villages, Barley, by way of what might have become London's third airport at Nuthampstead, now once again a quiet backwater.

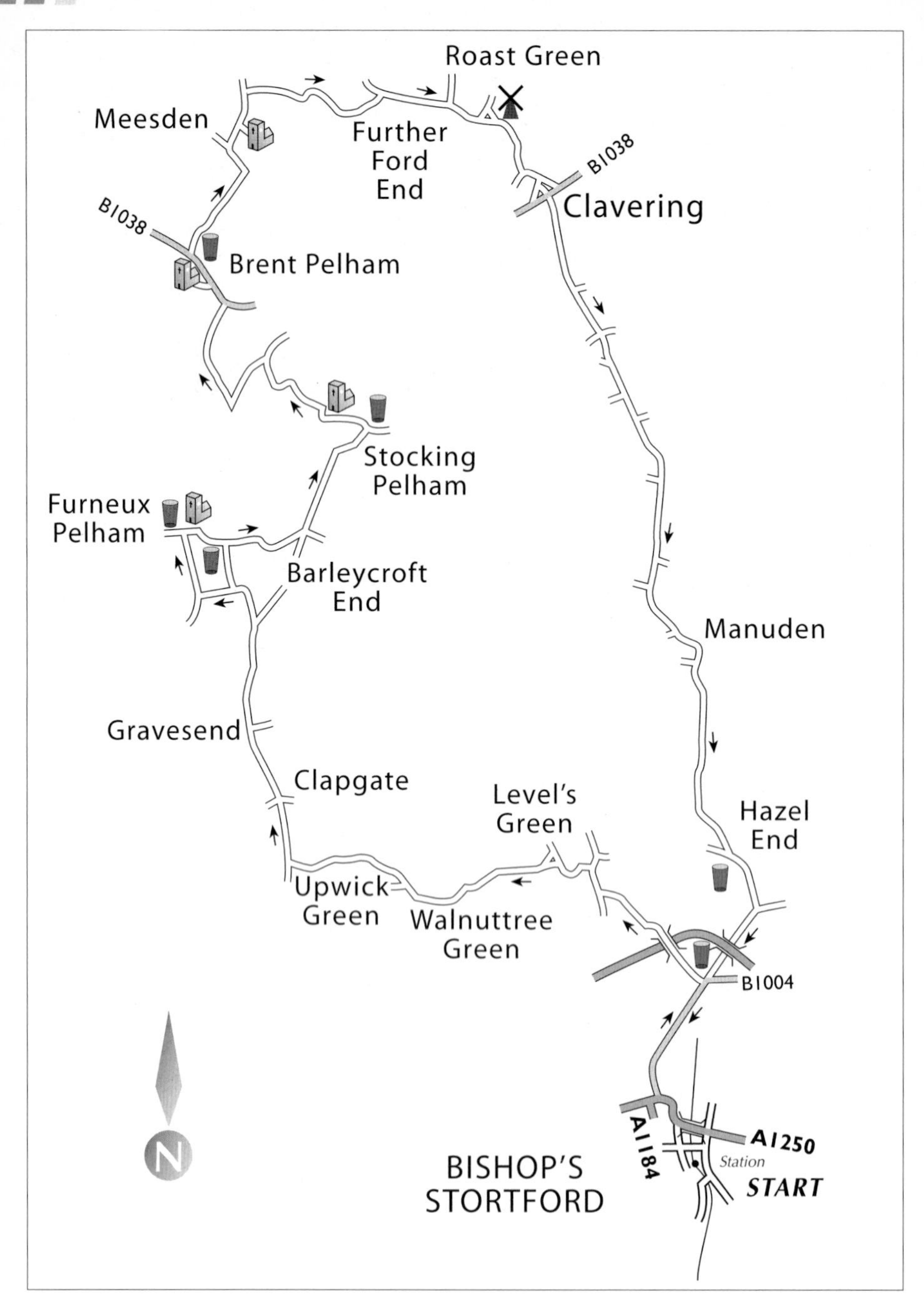
Roast Green
Meesden
Further
Ford
End
B1038
Clavering
B1038
Brent Pelham
Stocking
Pelham
Furneux
Pelham
Barleycroft
End
Manuden
Gravesend
Clapgate
Level's
Green
Hazel
End
Upwick
Green
Walnuttree
Green
B1004
A1250
A1184
Station
BISHOP'S
STORTFORD
START
N

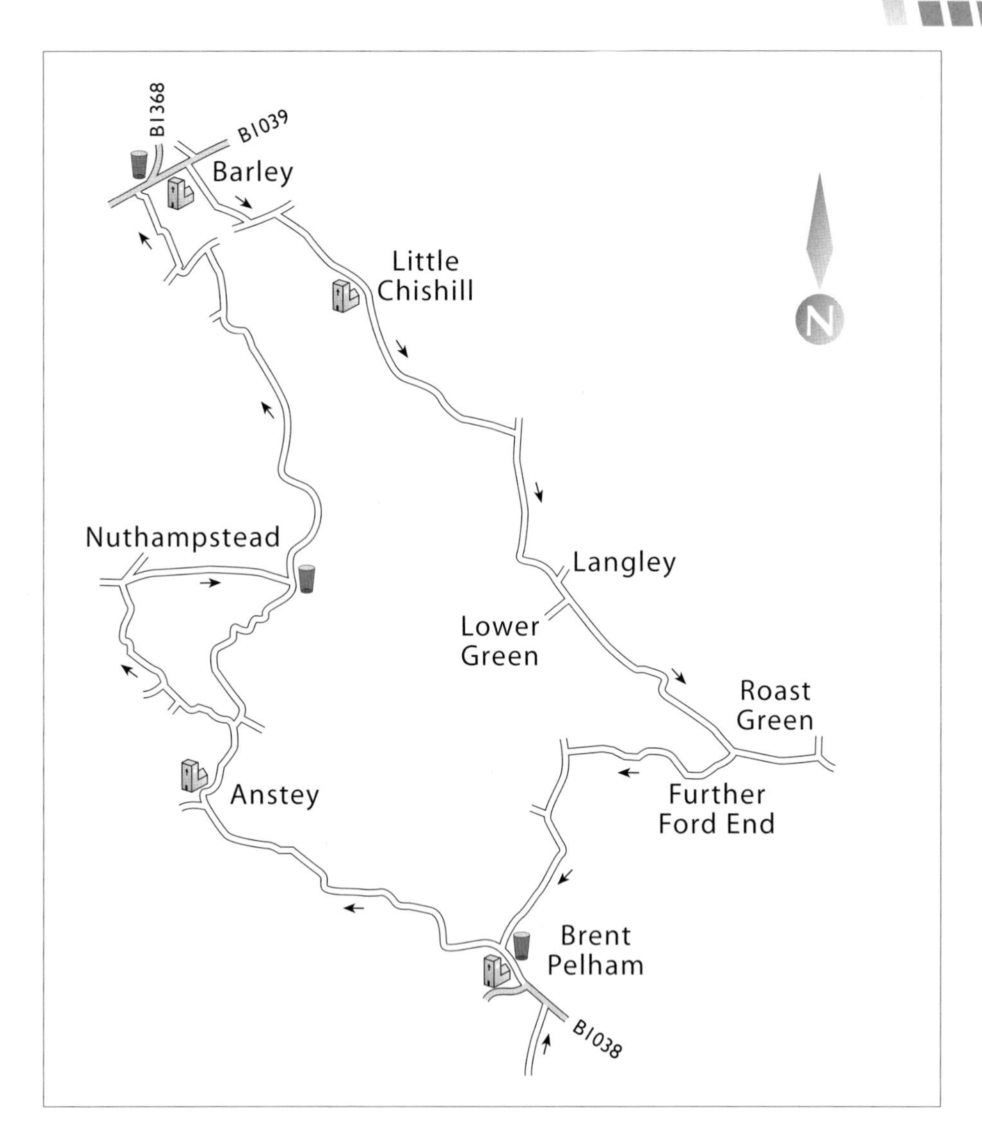

If you opt for this longer ride, and on a sunny summer day it is well worth the effort, keep left at the Black Horse pub and follow a delightful lane towards Anstey, **bearing R** into the village. Pass the Chequers pub and a fine well-head, where **turn L** for Nuthampstead. At a crossroads **turn R** into the village and, by the Woodman Inn, **bear L** towards Barley. **Keep L again** (going right will bring you out on the airfield!) These lanes seem particularly traffic free. At the next T-junction **turn L** and **next R** through Smiths End. At the B1368 **turn R** into the village, where take the **next R** under the sign of the

Fox and Hounds. Local history tells that there had once been a fox which escaped from hounds by hiding in the thatched roof of the original building, which was burnt down in 1950.

Take the **next R** signed, 'Little Chishill', **turn L** at the T-junction, cross the county boundary and take the **next R**, signed to Little Chishill and Langley. It is a stiff little climb up to the church, but from the top the trend is downhill most of the way back. Pass through Langley Lower Green, with its pretty thatched cottages, then follow the Clavering signs through Further Ford End and Roast Green, where you rejoin the shorter route.)

Turn R at the Black Horse in Brent Pelham towards Meesden and **next R** past the church. **Turn R** again to bring you to Further Ford End, then **turn R** to Roast Green.

Continue past the junction for Stickling Green, with the remains of a tower mill on the left, and **bear L** into Clavering. Take the road to the **right** through the ford (or over the footbridge) and cross straight over the B1038, signed 'Manuden'. There will soon be signs to Bishop's Stortford to encourage you.

From here is an excellent, almost straight country road, not quite flat, but easy to Manuden, another small town of old but well preserved houses, both half timbered and pargeted. The road continues through Hazel End, where **keep R** (it is really straight on) at the next junction, and again **R** at the Red, White and Blue pub. You are now on the B1004, and should recognise the way you left town. At the roundabout follow the town centre signs to the station or car parks.

NUTHAMPSTEAD

This quiet village became the site of a busy Second World War airfield in 1942. Its first operational unit was the 55th Fighter Group, in 1943, flying P38 Lightnings. Nuthampstead closed finally in 1959. There is a memorial to the American flyers, with the words 'Hell from Heaven', by the Woodman Inn. This airfield figures with twelve others in an interesting leaflet, *Bedford WWII Airfield Trail*, obtainable from Bedford TIC.

BRENT PELHAM

Although all three Pelhams have many buildings of note with interesting histories, only Brent Pelham has a cunning giant. In the north wall of the church is a 13th-century tomb of an unknown person about whom a legend has grown up. It is supposed to be the burial place of a medieval lord of the manor named Piers Shonks, who reputedly slew a dragon. This beast was under the protection of the Devil, who declared that he would possess Piers' immortal soul whether he was buried inside or outside the church. Piers left directions in his will that he should be buried half in and half outside the church, thus frustrating the plans of the Devil.

14

Sandy, Biggleswade and Old Warren

17 miles

Sandy, Bedfordshire, has put up with many jokes about its name, but it is quite straightforward, really. Sandy stands on a sandhill. The low, tree-clad hill of Sandy Warren, home to both a nature reserve and the headquarters of the Royal Society for the Protection of Birds, rises from the flat cabbage fields by the river Ivel, winding its way lazily from the Hertfordshire border to join the Great Ouse near Tempsford. This level countryside facilitates the route of the Great North Road, which has been a Mecca for speed-seeking cyclists since racing began, but will soon be so no more, as vehicle numbers drive us to the peace and comparative safety of the lanes. A short detour will take us to a reminder of one of cycling's 'greats'. Southwards we find another belt of low sandhills, this time containing a variety of interesting places to visit, from a Swiss garden to a falconry centre and a major assemblage of vintage aircraft – the Shuttleworth Collection.

Map: OS Landranger 153 Bedford & Huntingdon (GR 177487).

Starting point: Sandy railway station on the King's Cross, London to Peterborough line. There is free parking in the centre of Sandy. From the parking, which has toilets and a tourist office, turn left towards the station.

Refreshments: There are shops and cafés in Sandy, various public houses and small shops *en route* and refreshment facilities at the Shuttleworth Collection.

The route: We start with some easy off-road cycling and end with the biggest hill of the day, the footbridge over the A1! This countryside is generally very flat, with a few little rises and falls near Old Warden. The lanes are usually very quiet, although there may be traffic around Old Warden when there is a 'Flying Day' at the Shuttleworth Collection.

From the station **turn R** over the bridge and then immediately **R** onto Stratford Lane. Follow this lane round the foot of the hill at Sandy Warren until it turns into a broad track. When you reach a stone wall on the left, look out for a **R turn** on a bridleway going south towards Biggleswade. The path avoids mud and fallen trees by climbing up on the right-hand bank, but it is quite easy to negotiate. Cross a wooden bridge, not forgetting to shut the gate, and follow the broad grassy track across a huge field to another gate, to the

A delightful estate cottage, Old Warden

right of the buildings of Furzenhall Farm. **Bear R** on the track, then **L** and it becomes surfaced again. In the distance you can see the outskirts of Biggleswade. Go straight on to the residential road and **turn R** at the T-junction. Continue on the major road, over the railway and at the T-junction by the Rising Sun pub **turn R**. This is Sun Street.

Turn L at the end onto what was once the Great North Road and continue straight over at the next roundabout. Various shops and eating places are off to the left, but continue over two more roundabouts to pass under the new A1 to the **next right**, signed 'Broom, Scenic Route', out in the country once more. Shortly cross over the River Ivel on a double bend and beside the mill owned by a famous muesli company.

Carry on through Broom village, past the White Horse pub on the left of the rather pleasant green, then over the next crossroads with **care**, signed 'Southill'. Go through Southill village, passing a little stores and post office on the left; **turn R** at the crossroads by White Horse pub, signed for Old Warden. Keep left at the next junction, still on the Scenic Route. You are now in a thickly wooded area, a complete contrast to the flat agricultural land you have been

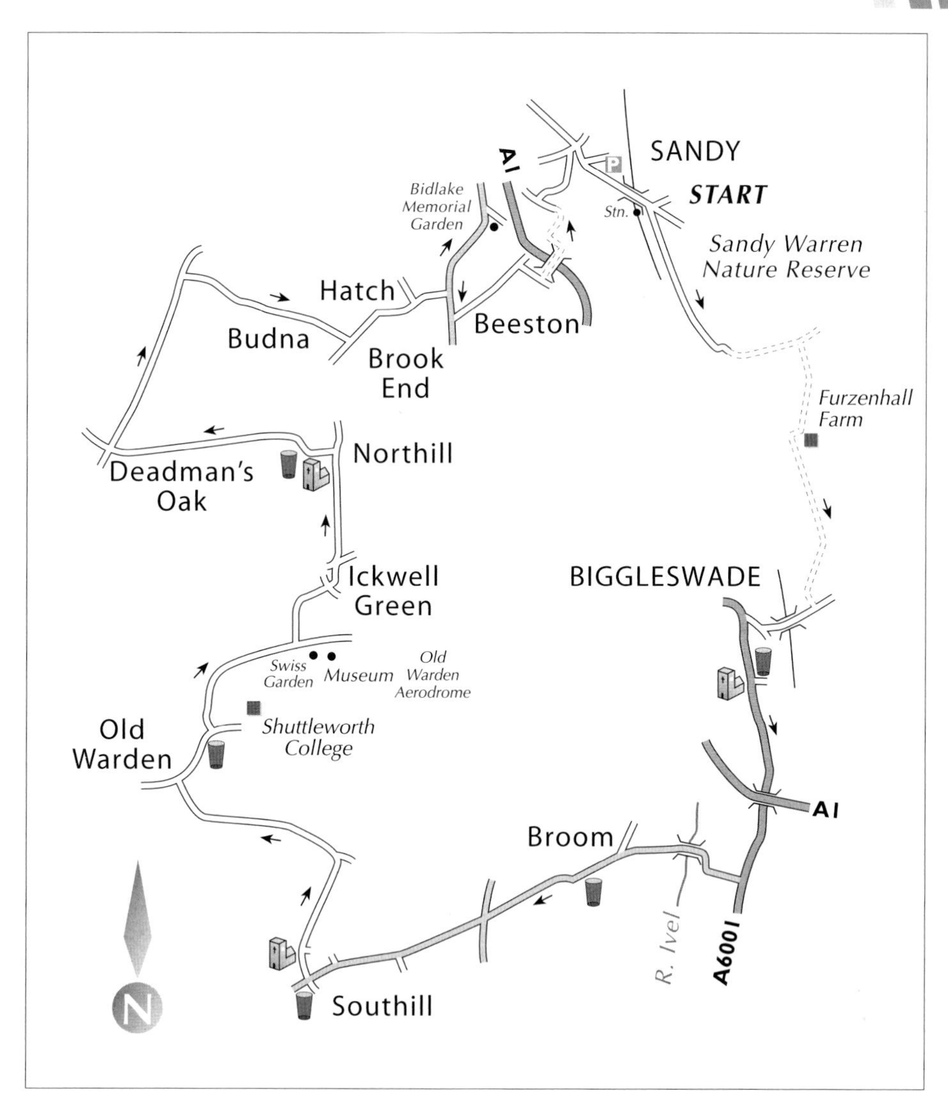

crossing and you will find a few little hills in this parkland round Old Warden. **Bear R** at the T-junction into the village with its rather picture postcard estate cottages. There is a post office on the right and the Hare and Hounds pub and a village pump on the left, at the bend by the entrance to Shuttleworth College, which is also the way in to the Shuttleworth Collection, the falconry centre and the Swiss Garden.

Continue past the church to the next junction. **Turn L** to Ickwell and Ickwell Green and carry straight on to Northill. **Turn L** after

The Bidlake Memorial

the pretty duckpond and the church on the left towards Cople. **Turn R** at the next crossroads, Deadman's Oak, signed 'Moggerhanger', and by a little copse **turn R** onto Budna Lane, a narrow, winding road, and at the end **turn L**, signed to Hatch, where go straight on to the T-junction at Brook End.

Turn L here for a detour of ½ mile and back to visit the Bidlake Memorial.

Almost a place of pilgrimage for the time-trialling cyclist is the Bidlake Memorial Garden, hiding in the fork at the junction of the B658 to Sandy and a remnant of the Great North Road, just south of Girtford Bridge. There is a memorial seat with his name, F T Bidlake, and a sundial with the words 'He measured Time'. He was a well-known racing man in his youth and a timekeeper in the heyday of racing on these local roads early last century. I would strongly discourage the use of the direct route into Sandy from here across the junction of the A1 and the Bedford road, so retrace your route to Brook End.

At Brook End **turn L** onto a lane marked 'Unsuitable for heavy vehicles' and in Beeston village

turn R at the village green. **Turn L** at a sign 'Greensand Walk' into The Crescent. At the end of The Crescent walk along the short path to the edge of the A1 and **go L** onto the ramp of the footbridge. This is not particularly cycle friendly, having shallow steps all the way up and down, but better and infinitely safer than trying to cross the dual carriageway. On the far side continue forward (northwards) on the pavement to the next **turn R**, now signed as Greensand footpath and bridleway. After crossing the river Ivel, **turn L** onto the road and immediately **R** onto Sunhill Gardens, but go carefully as the end is blocked off and you will have to pause and take to the pavement for a moment. **Turn R (with care)** at the end, then **R again** at the roundabout in Sandy. After the pedestrian lights and the next crossroads, the car park is on your left and the station a little further, on your right.

THE SHUTTLEWORTH COLLECTION

This is a collection of over forty aircraft, dating from 1909 to 1955. There are also vintage vehicles, motorcycles and bicycles in the collection. Unlike many aircraft museums, the planes in this one are still airworthy and about a dozen 'Flying Days' are held throughout the year. The collection includes a Bleriot Type XI, identical to the one which first crossed the Channel in 1909, and a Bristol Box Kite built for the film *Those Magnificent Men in their Flying Machines.*

The collection was started by Richard Shuttleworth in 1928, when he began to obtain early cars and aeroplanes to restore and use. His first aeroplane, a de Havilland Moth, bought in 1932 and four years old at the time, is still in the collection. Sadly Richard was killed in a flying accident in 1940 while serving with the RAF. Old Warden airfield was used for dismantling, rebuilding and flight testing during the war.

There are now eight hangars containing aircraft to be seen, as well as a nearby bird of prey centre and the Swiss garden, which is open Wednesdays, Thursdays and weekends. The collection is open from the New Year until just before Christmas. For details of 'Flying Days' and the other attractions at Old Warden Park: telephone: 01767 627288; fax 01767 626229; www.shuttleworth.org

RSPB

The Royal Society for the Protection of Birds, whose headquarters is at Sandy Lodge, is a registered charity and a major conservation organisation, both nationally and internationally. It owns bird reserves all over the country and encourages a healthy environment, the conservation of endangered species and the reintroduction of those almost lost to us, such as the amazingly successful red kite programme in the Chilterns. Membership provides funds for 'protecting the best' of our natural heritage and gives members the entry to over 100 bird reserves from Caithness to Cornwall and a quarterly magazine containing fascinating articles and the most wonderful bird photography. For details: telephone: 01767 680551; www.rspb.org.uk

15
North from Bedford

24 miles

The town centre of Bedford is better explored on foot to see its many links with John Bunyan and to enjoy its riverside walk. However, you can easily get out by bicycle, into the surrounding countryside to one of the pleasant local country parks and to seek out no less than three windmills. Bedfordshire is a small county, often regarded as flat and uninteresting or to be crossed on the way to somewhere else, but its villages can delight with cottages of local brick, weather-boarded or half-timbered and thatched. Its side roads are quiet and more rolling than you might expect. All you need to avoid is foggy weather, as the valley of the Great Ouse collects its grey blanket in the early hours of the morning and can hide in it all day!

Map: OS Landranger 153 Bedford & Huntingdon (GR 041497).

Starting point: Bedford Midland Road station on the King's Cross, London to Bedford line, in Ashburnham Road. There is plenty of parking in Bedford itself; that between River Street and Horne Lane is nearest to the station. Look for signs to the A428, Northampton to join the route.

Refreshments: Most public houses on the route offer food, but also there is a very pleasant café and picnic area in the Harrold Odell Country Park.

The route: You will not need very low gears for this ride, but do not be deceived, it is rarely flat. It crosses the river Great Ouse twice and follows its left bank towards Bletsoe, then it is up and down via Thurleigh and its once busy Second World War airfield, one more pretty lane then back into the town.

Turn L outside the station onto Ashburnham Road. At the roundabout **turn L** onto the A428, signed to Northampton. After crossing the railway there is a shared cyclepath on the right-hand side of the road (better than the one on the left, which soon ends). Shortly after the next roundabout follow this path into the **right turning to** Bromham.

Cross the fine old causeway and bridge over the River Great Ouse into Bromham village and **turn R**, signed 'Stevington', and **R again**, onto Village Road. This is a very winding road and comes into Stevington at Park End. Your first windmill is up a turning on the left. In the middle of Stevington is the Red Lion pub on the right, the Royal George on the left, with a

Harrold Odell Country Park

little cross between them. Continue straight on uphill in the direction of Turvey. At the next junction **turn L** towards Carlton and Harrold. Now it is downhill and straight on through Carlton, with the Royal Oak on your right. Again, you will cross the river Great Ouse on a 'Road liable to flooding', but there's a raised walkway on the left, should the worst happen. Cross the very narrow old bridge, then on your right is the entrance to Harrold Odell Country Park. The visitors' centre, toilets and café are on the left, also a pretty lakeside picnic spot. The café is open for breakfast, lunch and tea, from 9 am to 5.30 pm. From here you may take the gravelled bridleway straight ahead to Odell village, rejoining the road at the Bell pub, but it is liable to flooding at the far end, so, if in doubt, return to the road.

Continue to and take the next **R turn** to Little Odell. One of the stone and thatch cottages here boasts the name of Mad Dog! In Odell itself there is a fine stone church on the left. Stay on the road to Sharnbrook and at the T-junction in the village **turn R**, signed 'Milton Ernest'. On your left is a tempting cake shop offering morning coffee and afternoon tea. On the right is the Swan pub, and near a left-hand bend you may glimpse the next windmill.

Fork R by the Fordham Arms on the major road, then it is under the railway arch and past the Mill

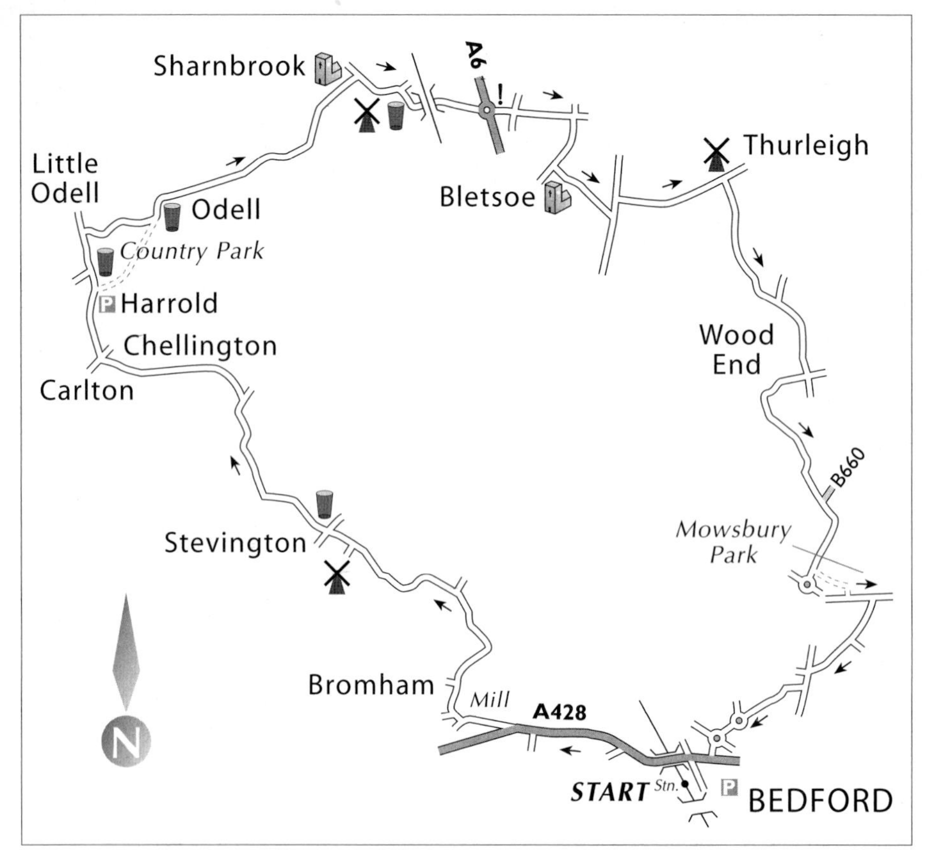

Theatre on the right to go straight over the roundabout, direction Thurleigh. At the second crossroads **turn R** towards Bletsoe village, where **turn L** by the church and **L** again, at the major road. Take the next **R** down a cutting, Milton Road, towards Thurleigh. Turn **next R** by the white windmill, now a handsome residence, through Scald End and continue to a **R turn**, signed 'Mon-Fri 7.30am to 9.0am No Right Turn except cycles'. **Turn R, with care**, down a pretty little lane – a house selling honey part way along – to rejoin the main road and **turn R** towards Bedford.

Just before the roundabout **turn L** on a cyclepath through Mowsbury Park, starting by the pedestrian lights, signed 'Bridleway'. Continue parallel to Westwood Drive to a mini-roundabout, where **turn R** onto the road into Putnoe Lane. Continue down Putnoe Lane, **bear L** at the traffic lights on Kimbolton Road, then **turn R** onto Park Avenue. After going straight over a little roundabout onto Ross Avenue, go straight over the next roundabout, heading for

The village of Harrold

Northampton, then **turn R** at the traffic lights on Bromham Road. **Turn L** at the mini-roundabout onto Ashburnham Road, and the station is on your right.

TWO MEN OF BEDFORD

John Howard, whose statue stands in Bedford close to St Paul's church, lived in Cardington and became High Sherriff of Bedfordshire in 1773. He noticed the poor state of the town's prisons and set out to make conditions more humane. One major cause of inhumanity was that the gaoler was not paid a fixed salary and often resorted to extortion. From Howard's research, two Parliamentary Bills were passed, one to pay gaol staff and the other to improve sanitation in prisons. He arranged for copies of these Acts to be sent at his own expense to all county gaols in England. After this he continued to press for prison reforms, spending considerable sums to secure them, and travelled widely to investigate and report on conditions, both at home and abroad. He died in 1789 in Russia.

Glenn Miller, the famous band leader, joined the United States Army, formed a new orchestra in 1943 and set about giving many concerts and broadcasts to raise money for the war effort. In 1944 he moved the whole show to London and then to the relative safety of Bedford. The band's first performance was given at Thurleigh airbase and its first broadcast from the Bedford Corn Exchange. It is said he particularly enjoyed British pubs and fish and chips. Following the liberation of Paris, General Eisenhower asked Glenn Miller to perform in Paris on Christmas Day. He was offered a lift on a private aircraft on 15th December. He took off from Twinwood airfield and was never seen again. It is thought the plane was brought down accidentally over the

Bromham's 17th century watermill

Channel by bombs off-loaded from a returning flight. There is now an exhibition in the original control tower at Twinwood and a memorial plaque at the Bedford Corn Exchange.

TWO MILLS

As you come into Bromham, its watermill stands by the Ouse on your right. It dates from the 17th century and has been restored to working order. It is possible to see milling in progress and buy various products. There are also other related events and exhibitions. It is open from March to October, Wednesday to Saturday, from 1 pm to 5 pm. For a free leaflet and details of open days, telephone: 01234 824330.

Just before Stevington village, look for its windmill on the left. This is a fine 18th-century post mill, the only complete one in Bedfordshire, and has fine views over the surrounding countryside. The keys may be obtained from the pubs in the village or telephone 01234 824330.

16
Ridgmont to Woburn

16 miles

An alternative title might be 'How the rich live' or 'Bedfordshire isn't all flat!' This is a fairly short ride to leave time for a visit to Woburn Abbey, home of the family of the Dukes of Bedford, currently the Marquis of Tavistock and his wife. It also takes a short tour around the wooded heights of Aspley and Wavendon Heaths. Apart from the abbey, Woburn has many handsome buildings, particularly its tourist information centre. The villages have stone cottages reminiscent of an iron-tinged Cotswold scene and the route round Woburn Park is enhanced by herds of many types of deer.

Maps: OS Landranger 153 Bedford & Huntingdon and 165 Aylesbury & Leighton Buzzard (GR 965373).

Starting point: Ridgmont station on the Bletchley to Bedford line. There is very little parking at Ridgmont station and it would be better for car travellers to join the circuit at Woburn, where there is free parking on the right of the road into the park and opposite the parish church.

Refreshments: There are numerous pubs and hotels in Woburn, mainly fairly expensive, but the Copperfield Tearooms also does light meals. There are refreshments at the abbey and the Green Man pub at Eversholt is good value.

The route: After a short stretch in the Bedfordshire plain, there is a testing climb up to Aspley Guise and the heathland above. From here the route into Woburn is easy and the parkland is gently rolling and should not be hurried. Although there are some interesting tracks through the heaths, they are very sandy and are not included in this route.

Turn L out of the station, over the level crossing, **turn L** at the roundabout and cross straight over the traffic lights on the A507, signed to Hulcote and Salford. Hulcote is tiny, just a house or two, a farm and a church, but Salford is more substantial. **Turn L** in Salford and pass the Swan pub on the right and the oddest little spiky-spired church on the left. Go through Salford ford, with the Red Lion hotel on your right, and over the M1 bridge, then take the **next L**, Crabtree Lane, signed 'Aspley Guise'. Now you are heading for the hills, perhaps the 'Delectable Mountains' in John Bunyan's *Pilgrim's Progress*.

Woburn Abbey, the family home of the Dukes of Bedford

It is a steady climb over the level crossing and up to the fine stone church in Aspley Guise. Then comes a brief respite in the village centre with its little market cross. Go straight over the crossroads past some unusual tall, thin, white houses and continue to climb. On the major road **bear R** at Gipsy Lane and **L** at Woodside. At the T-junction **turn L** onto the A5130 into Woburn.

The Woburn Heritage Trust Museum and Tourist Information Centre is on the right of the A5130, in the old church of St Mary, with its extremely decorated tower. It is open from Easter to October, Monday to Friday 2 pm to 4.30 pm, Saturdays, Sundays and bank holidays 10 am to 5 pm (weekends only in October). In the village you can also find shops, a post office and toilets. **Turn L** in the centre of the town towards the park. Opposite the car park, the parish church of St Mary has four extremely ugly figures looking over the top of the tower like upright gargoyles. There are seats opposite the church, which would serve for a picnic, as the tempting grass in the haha opposite is often wet!

Proceed into the park with lakes either side of the road and an abundance of huge trees and rhododendrons.

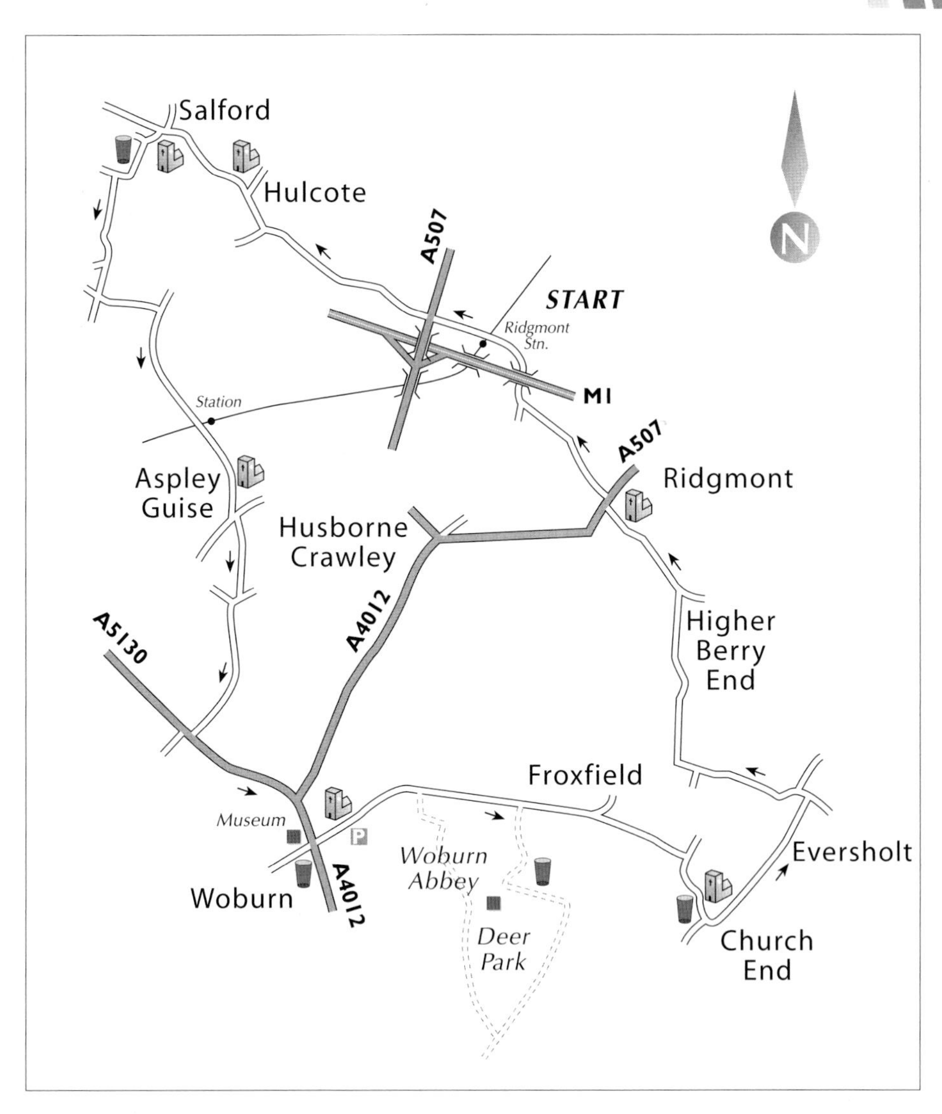

To visit the house **turn R** as directed and take the beautiful driveway circling the park among the herds of deer. From this you will get the best view of the front. Continue to the exit signs and **turn R** on the road to the gate. In winter it is always possible to take this route, but when the house is open it may be used only by those visiting it. Otherwise take the direct road through the park. (It is not possible to visit the Safari Park by bicycle.)

Go through the exit gate and **bear R**, signed 'Froxfield'. At the T-junction **turn R**, signed 'Milton

The village of Woburn

Bryan', past a beautifully preserved black and white cottage and follow the lane into Eversholt, the Green Man pub on the left and the church on the right. Take the **next L** signed to Church End, and **turn L** at the T-junction, signed 'Steppingly'. Keep **L** at the next junction, signed 'Woburn Abbey Park', and take the next **R** along Berry End, signed 'Ridgmont'. **Turn L** towards Ridgmont. At the A507 in the village **turn R** and immediately **L** to descend, passing under the M1, to Ridgmont station on the left.

WOBURN ABBEY

The present house stands on the site of a Cistercian monastery, founded by Hugh de Bolebec in 1145. Nothing of this now remains and the magnificent building seen today is the work of Henry Flitcroft, who rebuilt it in 1746. The first of the Russell family to own the abbey was John, 1486–1555, who was made a Baron by Henry VIII and Earl of Bedford by his son Edward VI. His great grandson Francis was instrumental in employing the Dutch engineer, Vermuyden, to drain the fens. Today the abbey remains the family home and also houses one of the finest art collections in the country, including works by Reynolds and Gainsborough and a whole roomful of Canaletto's views of Venice, as well as collections of silver, gold and porcelain.

17

Leighton Buzzard – the Greensand Ridge

21 miles

The countryside around Leighton Buzzard shows a wide variety of features caused by its geological position on the borders of chalk, clay and sand. The town itself has expanded since the arrival of the mainline railway and the Grand Union Canal, taking the easy route north. Its industries have profited from the commercial exploitation of the sand, which is the reason for the narrow gauge line and which also supports the scenic heathland enjoyed by the cyclist. Southwards the views to the Chilterns are rewarding.

Map: OS Landranger 165 Aylesbury & Leighton Buzzard (GR 911250).

Starting point: Leighton Buzzard station, on the Euston, London to Milton Keynes line. There is plenty of parking in town, signed from the central roundabout.

Refreshments: Leighton Buzzard and many of the villages have pubs which cater and Eaton Bray has a choice of three, one of the favourites with club cyclists being the Hope and Anchor in Eaton Bay. The café in Stockgrove Country Park is also popular.

The route: Once out of town, it traverses the level area of the headwaters of the River Ouzel towards the Chiltern hills, but turns short, avoiding their outlier at Totternhoe, to a little climb after the railway crossing and the longer drag up into the sandhills towards Great Brickhill, from where there is plenty of downhill back to Leighton Buzzard.

Turn L outside the station, then **half R** on Old Road and **R again**, still on Old Road, straight down to the traffic lights, where go straight across. **Turn R (care)** into the town centre. The sign to Town Centre and Church Square is not very easy to see, but look out for Dorvics Cycles high up on the wall in front of you by the junction. Cyclists can continue straight through on the line of the old High Street. Note the handsome church and some major civic offices. **Turn R** at the end and continue to the mini-roundabout on the Stanbridge Road, where **turn L** (unless you want to visit the Leighton Buzzard Light Railway, once the transport for the sand quarries, which is straight on for about ¼ mile on the A4146 and well signed).

After a level crossing keep on the

The handsome pub in Great Brickhill

major road, which goes right and then left at the two mini-roundabouts, then **bears R**, signed Billington. **Turn L and immediately R** on the dual carriageway A505 **(care)**. Pass The Meads Open Farm on your right and take the **next L**, the Rye, signed to Eaton Bray, shortly before reaching Billington. **Turn R** at the next junction into Eaton Bray. The Five Bells pub is on the right, as is the needle-spired church. Keep straight on past the Hope and Anchor pub on your left, then take the **second turn left** at a crossroads, the narrow Doolittle Lane. There is a really good view of the Whipsnade Lion chalk carving on the slope of Dunstable Downs ahead and the lumpy outline of Five Knolls a bit to the left.

Turn L past the tower of Doolittle Mill. **Turn R** at the next junction and follow the lane to Totternhoe Church End, where **bear L** into Totternhoe village. On the left is the Old Farm Inn and on the right the steep path up to Totternhoe Knolls Nature Reserve. It positively looms over the village. On your left is the Cross Keys pub. Follow the major road through Lower End. At a T-junction **turn R** and immediately **left** onto the A505, **then first right (care)**, making for Stanbridge.

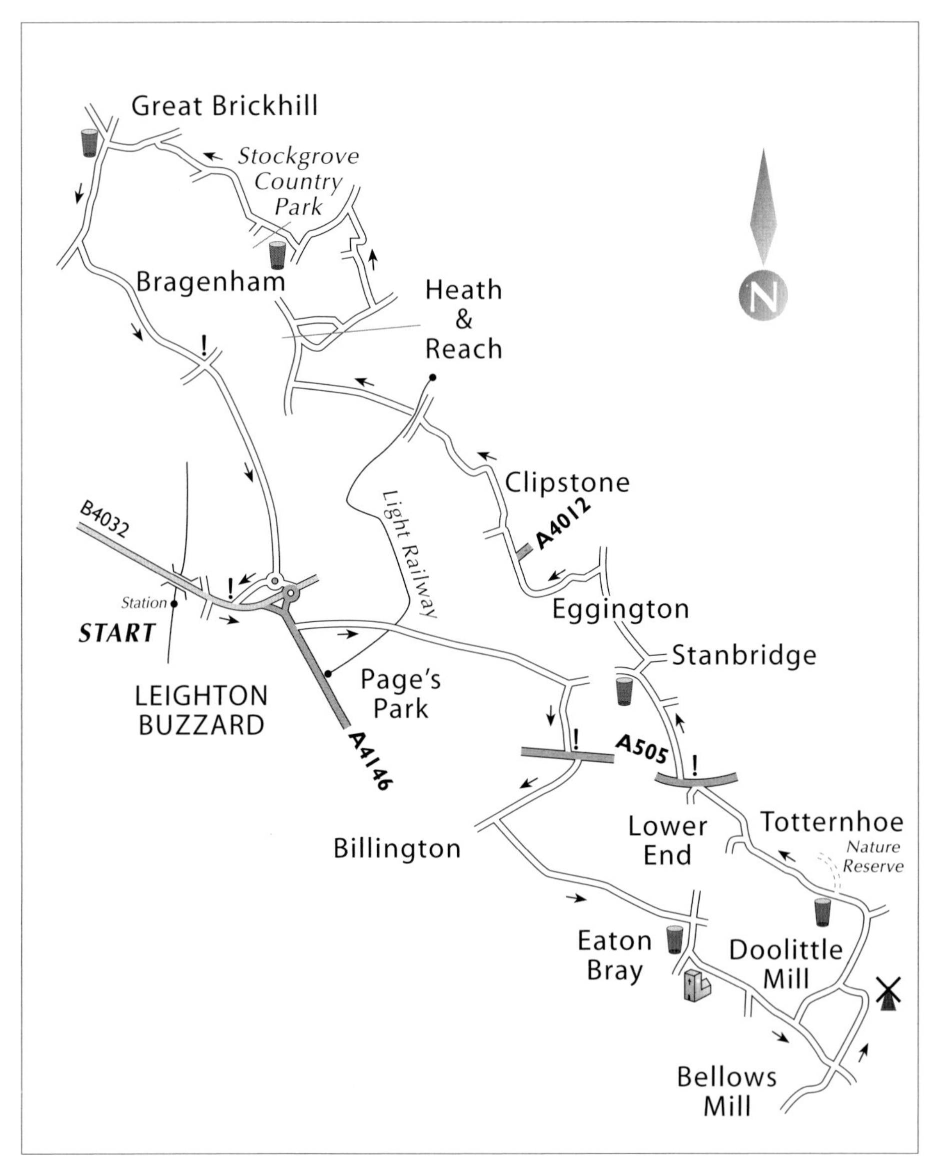

Continue through Stanbridge to the give way sign, where **turn R** for Eggington beside the rather up-market Five Bells pub and restaurant. Opposite the church **turn L** (the sign is tucked away on your side of the road) and climb up past another defunct tower mill, to descend and **turn L** through Eggington. Follow the winding road through the village to the main road, the A4012, which you join (straight on) and take the **next R (care)**, signed 'Clipstone'.

The Whipsnade Lion, carved in the Downs

Continue to the next crossroads, where you go straight over, also over a level crossing on the light railway. Climb up Shenley Hill Road and down again. You can see a sand quarry on your right, showing a good many variations in colour. At the T-junction **turn R** and **R** again after the church in Heath and Reach. Take the **second turn L**, shortly after passing a water tower. There are some cottages along here built of the local greensand stone. At the fork keep right and **turn L** at the T-junction onto the main road. At the bottom of the winding hill take the **next R**, signed Great Brickhill. Climb a little, then descend to the entrance to Stockgrove Country Park on the left. Unfortunately you cannot cycle in the park, but there is a useful snack bar/café and plenty of picnic space.

From here the lane winds uphill to Great Brickhill. At the T-junction, opposite a display of sarsen stones, the Old Red Lion pub is facing you – a pub with a view! **Turn L** here and descend to the **next turn L**, Bragenham Lane – more views to the right over the valley of the River Ouzel, but take care on the descent of the narrow lane. Another up and down brings you to a tricky crossroads with rather poor visibility. Cross straight over **(care)** into Plantation Road. At a junction by the Stag pub, **bear R** and at the next roundabout **turn R** back to the traffic lights and follow the signs to the station.

LEIGHTON BUZZARD RAILWAY

The particularly pure sand found under the clay layer around Leighton Buzzard has been quarried industrially since the 18th century. It is used in many industries, from foundries to building golf course bunkers, and, in the past, to make some of the glass for the Crystal Palace. It is so famous and specialised, it has even been exported to the Sahara! This reconstructed narrow gauge line was originally opened in 1919 to transport sand from the quarry, after complaints about damage to roads. It carried up to 20 trainloads of sand a day during the 40s and 50s, but its use declined shortly afterwards, re-opening for passengers in 1968. There is a major collection of narrow gauge locomotives as well as a shop. The line is 5½ miles long but only 4¾ miles is currently in use and the round journey takes some 65 minutes from Page's Park station. It is open every Sunday, including bank holidays, from 10 am to 4 pm with various other special opening times. Telephone: 01525 373888 for further information.

EATON BRAY

The 'place by the river' belonging to the Bray family once had a castle, now marked only by the name Castle Field at Park Farm, west of the village. Sir Reginald Bray, lord of the manor in 1490, was both a statesman and an architect, being High Treasurer and Chancellor of the Duchy of Lancaster and the builder of St George's Chapel at Windsor. He also added to the local church, which dates from around 1220 and still contains two of the long hooked poles used to remove burning thatch from cottage roofs.

18

Flitwick and Wrest Park

22 miles

The Greensand Ridge area of Bedfordshire has provided the rich brown stone for the handsome, chunky village churches of the area. It nestles between the chalk hills of the Chilterns and the clay vale of the Great Ouse, providing a well drained land of forest and field and a firm base for a series of small towns and villages from Ampthill (meaning 'anthill!) to Shefford. For the cyclist there is plenty of scope with only very moderate hills, some well drained trails, several places of historical interest and links with John Bunyan. It is a pity there is no station at Ampthill, a town with a fine main street, a park and a nature reserve, but it may be better explored on foot, so the more urban Flitwick must suffice for start and finish.

Map: OS Landranger 153 Bedford & Huntingdon (GR 033350).

Starting point: Flitwick station on the King's Cross, London to Bedford line. There is car parking on the right beside the railway in the road towards Greenfield, just after the start of the route.

Refreshments: As is usually the case in this area, most public houses – and there are plenty of them – cater for lunchtimes. Shefford has a choice of pubs, shops and other food outlets, while there are picnic opportunities on the John Bunyan Trail.

The route: The off-road (about 4½ miles) is clear and firm based and the road sections undulating, but not really testing. It is generally traffic free once you leave the area of the station, with just a couple of crossings requiring care.

Turn L outside Flitwick station, **L** again over the railway and immediately **R**, signed 'Greenfield'. Pass the Crown pub on the right, follow the major road round to the left, then **turn R** at a T-junction onto Greenfield Road. There is a fine old weather-boarded watermill on the right. At the next T-junction **turn L** to go straight through Greenfield towards Flitton. In Flitton the White Hart pub is on the left facing the church, which contains a well preserved mausoleum of the de Grey family, who lived at Wrest Park, Silsoe. It is said to be one of the best collections of funerary memorials in the country, dating from a brass of 1545 up to the 19th century. Outstanding is the monument to Henry de Grey and his two wives,

The pub in Flitton

dating from 1740. The key is available at any reasonable time from Mr J Stimson, 3 Highfield.

Now keep right at the fork on Wardhedges Road and **turn L** at the Jolly Coopers, signed 'Silsoe', then **R** at the next junction, **R** again onto Vicarage Road and **L** at the end, coming into the centre of Silsoe opposite the church and the entrance to Wrest Park. There is a shop, a restaurant and a pub to the left in Silsoe, but the route continues straight through the park on the driveway in front of the mansion.

The bridleway climbs towards Upper Gravenhurst. At the road **turn R** and next **L** through the village and **L** again, signed to Campton, with the Green Dragon pub on the left. In Campton **turn L** past the church and just before the A507 take the cyclepath on the right, which passes underneath to come out on the main street in Shefford. **Turn R** into the town centre. The Bridge pub is ahead and 'Fresh Baked Pies' on your left, also fish and chips. Go straight on at the mini-roundabout to the traffic lights by the White Hart, where **turn L**, signed to Sandy. (There are toilets on the left here.) Once over the river Flit, **turn L** towards Bedford, the White Swan pub on your right.

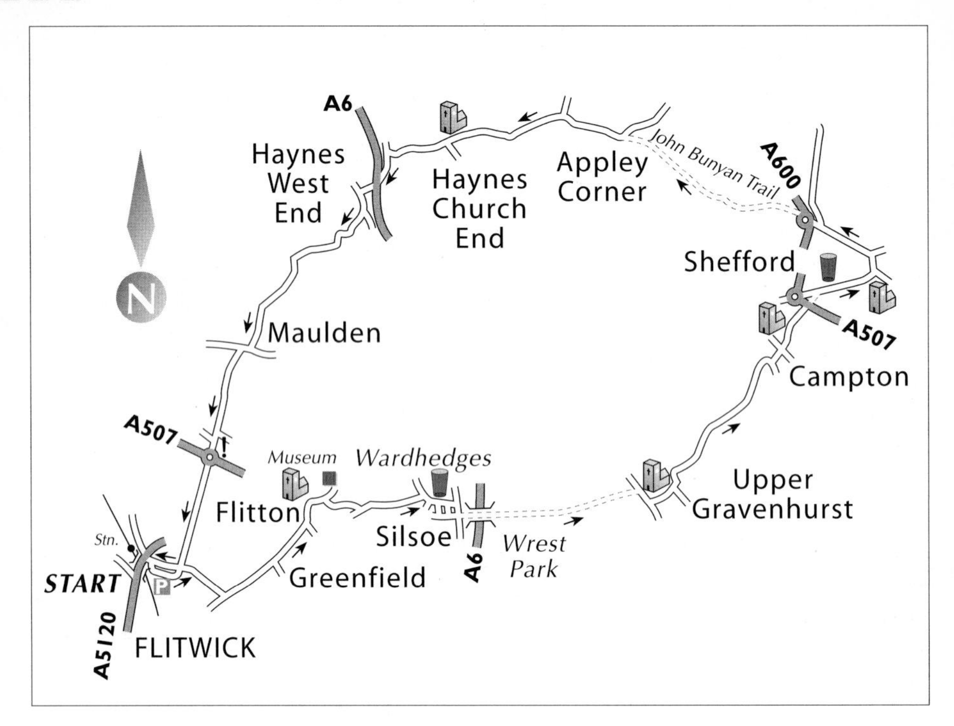

At the A600 go straight over the roundabout onto the bridleway, which is part of the John Bunyan trail (a long off-road cycle route to Elstow, near Bedford, which was Bunyan's birthplace). The trail meets the road again at Appley Corner, where **turn L**.

Keep straight on to Haynes Church End, past Haynes Park mansion, to the junction with the A6. **Turn L and first R**, with **great care**, towards Haynes West End. **Bear L and R**, signed 'Maulden'. At the bottom of the hill in Maulden **turn R** and almost immediately **L** into Flitwick Road. Cross the A507 **with care** at the roundabout, signed 'Flitwick Industrial Estate' – not the most beautiful entry into town, but it is a straightforward route. At the T-junction **turn R** onto Kings Road. Then it is **R and L** over the railway and **R** to the station.

WREST PARK

This is now the Silsoe Institute, but is a late 17th-century mansion, designed by Sir William Chambers, with formal gardens laid out by 'Capability' Brown amongst others. The 90 acres of formal gardens, lakes, woodland walks and picnic areas are open to the public from 1st April to 31st October, 10 am to 6 pm, weekends and bank holidays (open until 5 pm in October).

THE JOHN BUNYAN TRAIL

The track which leads from the north-western outskirts of Shefford in the direction of Bedford is named after the

Wrest Park

county's most famous son, the author of *The Pilgrim's Progress* and a religious reformer and preacher, imprisoned in Bedford jail for his beliefs. The track itself ends at Elstow, close to his birthplace at Harrowden. He was the son of a tinker and travelled the district with his father, returning to Elstow in his 20s. After the Civil War ended, he became interested in religion and moved into Bedford, where he began preaching. Laws were made forbidding preaching and Bunyan, determined to continue, was arrested at Harlington and imprisoned in the county gaol, where he spent the next twelve years. This gave him plenty of time to write. Finally released in 1677, he continued writing as well as travelling and preaching and teaching. He died in London in 1688. As well as his statue and museum in Bedford, there are many other sites in the county linked with him and his writings. An excellent free leaflet is available from the Tourist Information Centre, St Paul's Square, Bedford. Telephone: 01234 215226.

19

Harlington and the 'Delectable Mountains'

17 miles

The mountains of John Bunyan's *The Pilgrim's Progress* may have looked pretty high from the 'House Beautiful' (Houghton House, near Ampthill), but, fortunately for us, they rise only to some 500 feet. They are the outliers of the Chiltern hills, rearing up above the clay vale of the river Flit, the same clay that made Bedfordshire famous for its brickfields. Today, with most of the chimneys gone and the brickworks closed, we can climb the hills for the rural view from Sharpenhoe Beacon (or Sharpenhoe Clappers as the National Trust area is called). On this route the climb is optional, as it is quite tough, but apart from the view, you will be rewarded by good picnic spots and an exciting descent afterwards.

Maps: OS Landranger 166 Luton & Hertford and 153 Bedford & Huntingdon (GR 035304).

Starting point: Harlington station on the King's Cross, London to Bedford line. There is some parking at the station and there is also a small parking area at the top of the hill near Upper Sundon, but of course starting the route from there means climbing the hill at the end of the ride.

Refreshments: There is scope for a picnic with a view at the top of the hills at Sundon or at Sharpenhoe Clappers. The route passes a good many public houses offering a wide choice of menus, particularly in Barton-le-Clay, now quiet and bypassed, but once a busy little town catering for travellers on the A6 from London to Bedford and the north.

The route: The hill up to Upper Sundon is quite long and steep, but it is quiet and walking makes it easier. The descent to Sharpenhoe should be treated with respect, but again it is a quiet road. The rest of the ride is a potter through the villages, with one last little sting in the tail up to Pulloxhill.

(To avoid the hill climb, but enjoy a view of the hills, cross straight over the crossroads after the station and follow the winding road out of the village direct to Sharpenhoe village.)

Leaving the station, **turn R** over the bridge, up Station Road and **turn R with care** at the crossroads by the war memorial. It is a rather awkward turn, signed 'Sundon'. The winding road heads for the

Harlington

hills and the big climb. At the top on the left is the Sundon Hills Country Park, just a little parking area with an interesting board describing the John Bunyan Trail. There is a good view from here of Sharpenhoe Knoll and the valley of the river Flit.

On the outskirts of Upper Sundon **turn L** onto Streatley Road, past the timbered White Hart pub, and at the next junction **bear L** for Streatley. In that village **turn L**, signed to Sharpenhoe. Just before the descent, on the right is the entrance to Sharpenhoe Clappers, viewpoint and nature reserve, ideal for walking, but with no cycling facility. The huge water tower in the distance is at Pulloxhill.

Check your brakes and drop down the hill with **care** to Sharpenhoe village, where **turn R** by the Lynmore pub towards Barton-le-Clay.

Cross the bridge over the bypass into Barton-le-Clay and **turn L** onto the Bedford road, with the Royal Oak on the right and the Bull on the left, then the Waggon and Horses. Continue over a roundabout, then I would recommend crossing onto the shared cyclepath on the right-hand side of the road to **turn R** onto Higham Road without having to negotiate the large roundabout at the junction with the bypass. Pass the sturdy stone church of Higham Gobion on your left; the tower of

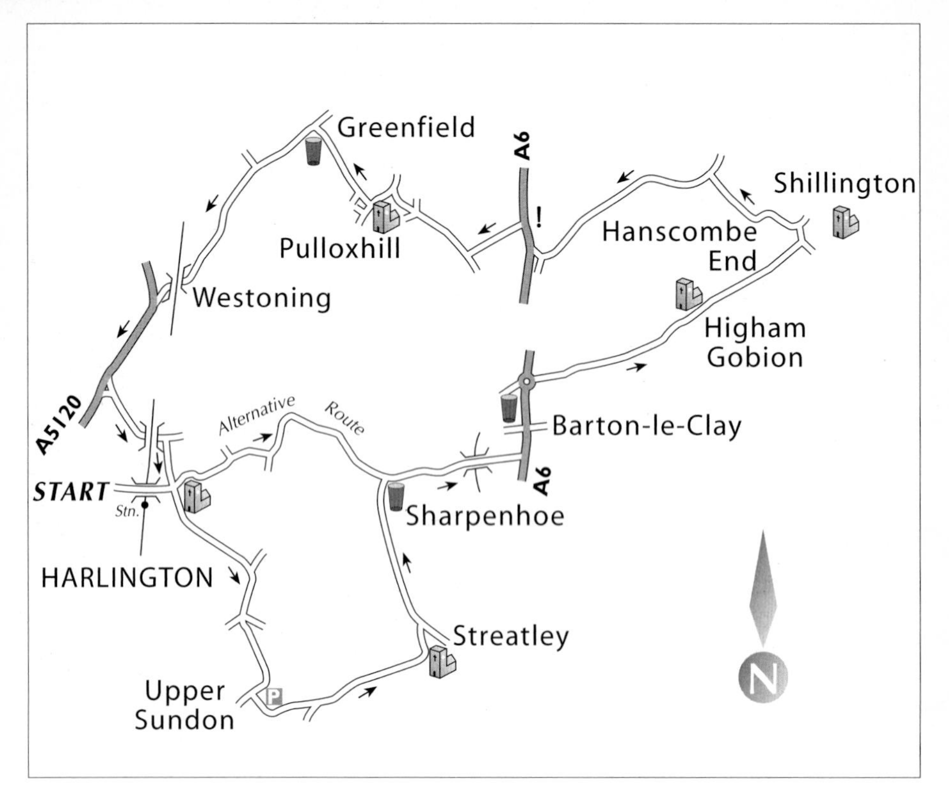

Shillington church can be seen ahead. These sandstone church towers are a feature of this area. On the outskirts of Shillington **turn L** for Hanscombe End. **Keep L** at the next junction on a narrow lane to a T-junction, where **turn L**, signed 'Pulloxhill'. Take the next **fork R** and at the A6 **turn R** onto the shared path on the right-hand side for a short distance towards Silsoe and **walk with care** across the main road into the next left turning, signed 'Pulloxhill'. **Turn R** at the next T-junction, at Kitchen End, and climb up the sharp little pitch to Pulloxhill; the Cross Keys pub and a village shop are on the right at the top. **Bear L** and then **R**, onto Greenfield Road.

Turn L through Greenfield towards Westoning, the Compasses pub on your left and a good mix of ancient and modern housing from converted barns and old thatch to modern infill. Go under the railway arch and past the Nag's Head and the Bell on the right, to **turn L** in Westoning village onto the sometimes busy A5120 towards Dunstable. Take the **next L**, signed to Harlington, **L again**, continue to go under the railway and **immediately R**, signed to Sundon. At the top of the rise, by the

Village sign

Carpenter's Arms, **turn R** onto Station Road. The station is on your left. (To retrace to the hilltop car park, keep straight on at the Carpenter's Arms.)

BARTON-LE-CLAY

Known since at least 1535 as Barton in the Clay, its name describes its situation perfectly. Set below the chalk outliers of Sharpenhoe and the Barton Hills, it served long as a staging post on the A6 between London and Bedford, the road climbing to over 400 feet in Bartonhill Cutting. The church of St Nicholas has a good nave roof and other items of interest, but the village was once known for a particularly fine straw grown for the plaiting industry, which in the early 1800s was a mainstay of the Bedfordshire economy. Luton was the centre of straw-hat making and in villages round about children, in particular, were employed long hours at home splitting and plaiting straw for some 2 or 3 shillings a week at age four to about 12 shillings a week at age nine to supplement the miserable agricultural wage their parents earned.

PULLOXHILL

Here is an unassuming village with two small claims to fame. One local field name is Gold Close, which commemorates the finding in 1680 of gold-bearing quartz, as far as I know, the only such find in Bedfordshire. The Crown immediately claimed it, but the amount turned out to be negligible. Another field name is Bunions Hill, referring to land held here by the Bunion family in the 13th century. It would seem probable that this family were ancestors of John Bunyan of Bedford. Field names can be a most interesting study in a modern parish, giving leads to the history of the place and links with farming and other usage.

20 Baldock to Ashwell

21 miles

It is an interesting place name, Baldock, derived from the Old French 'Baldac' for Baghdad, from its foundation in the 12th century by the Knights Templar. There is plenty to see in Baldock itself, from its fine 14th century church to its Georgian mansions, but these delights are best sought on foot. Our route is out into the borders of Bedfordshire and Cambridgeshire escaping from the town bustle into huge fields and remote villages, with Ashwell as its crowning delight.

Map: OS Landranger 153 Bedford & Huntingdon (GR 246343).

Starting point: Baldock Station on the King's Cross, London to Cambridge line. It is also possible to park fairly easily in Baldock, with ample space at the supermarket in the old, art deco Kayser Bondor factory building at the southern end of town.

Refreshments: The farm shop and café after crossing the A1 makes a good stop, but it might be as well to make for one of the several eating places in Ashwell to give yourself time to look round the village.

The route: Most of the route is over very level roads, open to the fine views, but also open to the winds, with few woods or hedges in this arable area to break their force. Choose a calm, clear day and the views are terrific, particularly as you will find a few rolling uplands towards the end of the ride. The hill from Ashwell to Bygrave comes as a bit of a shock to the system, but a mere 300 feet above sea level feels like the top of the world. There is a very busy road crossing about four miles out of Baldock; if you feel at all insecure or have novice riders with you, please take the alternative on the A507, which is rarely very busy.

From Baldock station **turn R** and cross the A507* diagonally right into Icknield Way. On a bend **turn R** under the railway onto Norton Road, past the Orange Tree pub and across the bridge over the A1(M). **Turn R** at a T-junction, signed 'Stotfold'. As you come into the 'ancient town' of Stotfold take the cyclepath on the **R** just before the roundabout crossing of the A507, which will take you under the main road and into town. At the next mini-roundabout **turn L** towards Astwick. There are plenty of shops, pubs and food outlets in Stotfold, including the Sunshine Café, a choice of two fish and chip shops and hot pies. At traffic lights by a chapel **turn R**, signed to

The unusual church of St Margaret of Antioch, Bygrave

Astwick. Once out of the built up area you come to Astwick, with some fine wooden barns with corrugated iron roofs. Perhaps they once were thatched. Over to the left the huge water tower on Topler's Hill rears up, a landmark on the A1. This is the busy road-crossing mentioned above. **Walk, with great care**, across the A1. There is a wide central reservation and good visibility, but traffic can be moving very fast! Once across the A1, in the lane to Hinxworth, there is a farm shop and tearoom on your right.

*(Alternatively, to avoid crossing the A1, **turn R** onto the A507 outside Baldock station, continue for 1½ miles, **turn R (care)** towards Newnham, **turn R** towards Ashwell and **turn L** at the edge of the village to rejoin the route at Hinxworth.)

Continue towards Hinxworth, the most northerly Hertfordshire village, with its fine old house, Hinxworth Place, and its little church, an attractive jumble of architecture, on your right. **Turn L** at the T-junction, signed 'Edworth', passing the little war memorial clock tower on your right and the Three Horseshes pub on the left.

Edworth is almost too small to be

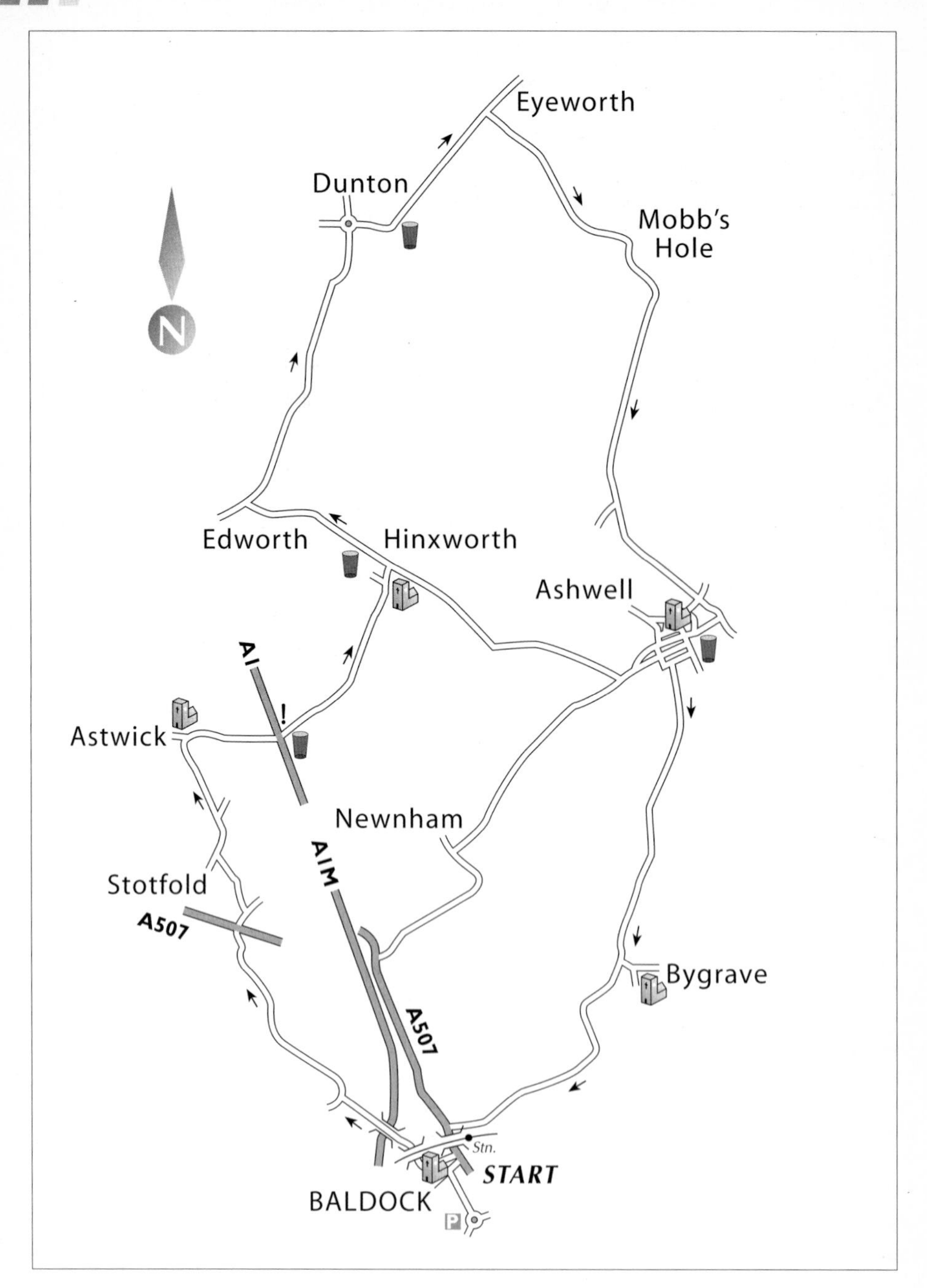
Eyeworth
Dunton
Mobb's Hole
N
Edworth
Hinxworth
Ashwell
AI
Astwick
Newnham
AIM
Stotfold
A507
A507
Bygrave
Stn.
START
BALDOCK
P

Hinxworth church

seen, just a little church and manor house off to the left. At the T-junction **turn R**, signed 'Dunton'. There are more wide views as this road is on a slight ridge. At a roundabout **turn R** for Dunton and Eyeworth. In Dunton on the right is the March Hare pub near the church and a post office stores on the left.

Just short of Eyeworth take a **R turn**, signed 'Ashwell', and drop down to Mobb's Hole, just a house near a bend by a stream, a headwater of the river Cam, which is the county boundary with Hertfordshire, while Cambridgeshire is only a few yards away. The map shows 'Moats' on the left, but no sign of historic buildings. Continue on the flat open road towards Ashwell, its tall tower with its lantern and spike on top dominating the village (you will have been able to see it in the distance for much of the ride). Keep left at a fork and at a T-junction **turn R** and immediately **R again** into the village.

There is so much to see in Ashwell, it merits a complete section of its own, but the route through the village **bears R** past the watermill, now desirable private residences, uphill past the church on the left to the museum, then **R** and **L** into the High Street, past a baker's and confectioner's providing takeaway food, then **L** takes you into Springhead. Retrace your route along the High Street to **turn L** past the Three Tuns, signed 'Bygrave'. **Turn R** at the crossroads and **L** again onto Bygrave Road and climb the long hill out of Ashwell.

Once at the top the road leaps down again, crosses the Cat Ditch and climbs again to Bygrave. Spare a few moments to visit Bygrave's unusual church of St Margaret of Antioch, a short way down a turning to the left. It has a Norman doorway, a 15th-century font, poppy-head benches and a rare 17th-century hourglass stand. Behind the church are earthworks, possibly of ancient British origin. Return to the road on which you entered Bygrave and resume the direction.

The road romps downhill, over another little rise and comes into Baldock between some of the purpose-built smallholdings that seem to be a feature of the outskirts of the town. At the A507 **turn L**, under the railway and immediately **L** again to the station.

ASHWELL

The size of the church illustrates the importance and prosperity of the village in the past as much as the preservation of the fine old houses proclaims it now. Inside, however, it is very plain. Opposite the church is a substantial old house with a plaque proclaiming it as a school built by the Merchant Taylors Company in 1681 and 'Mr Henry Colbron, late of London, Scrivener, deceased'.

At Springhead is the little garden where the River Rhee gushes from several springs, the source of the river Cam, and tempting stepping stones cross the infant stream. Otherwise there is a great range of beautiful old buildings to admire.

ASHWELL MUSEUM

The museum is open Sundays and bank holidays from 2.30 pm to 5 pm. It is a 15th-century building containing the office from which the Abbot of Westminster collected the Ashwell tithes. As it is in the market square it is probable that it was used for market business. It has been a meeting place for parish councillors and constables, a straw-plaiting school, an early meeting place for nonconformists, a tailor's shop and, until 1925, a dwelling. In 1930 it was restored and presented to Ashwell as a village museum by Sir William Gentle. It now houses an interesting collection of domestic items linked with the village and surrounding area.